Adolescent Suicide: Recognition, Treatment and Prevention

Adolescent Suicide: Recognition, Treatment and Prevention

Edited by
Barry Garfinkel, MD
Gorden Northrup, MD

The Haworth Press
New York • London

Adolescent Suicide: Recognition, Treatment and Prevention has also been published as *Residential Treatment for Children & Youth*, Volume 7, Number 1 1989.

The Haworth Press, Inc., 10 Alice Street, Binghamton, NY 13904-1580
EUROSPAN/Haworth, 3 Henrietta Street, London WC2E 8LU England

Library of Congress Cataloging-in-Publication Data

Adolescent suicide : recognition, treatment, and prevention / Gordon Northrup, Barry Garfinkel, editors.
    p. cm.
    "Has also been published as Residential treatment for children and youth, volume 7, number 1, 1989" — T.p. verso.
    Includes bibliographical references.
    ISBN 0-86656-949-9
    1. Suicide — Psychological aspects. 2. Teenagers — Suicidal behavior. 3. Adolescent psycho-therapy. I. Northrup, Gordon. II. Garfinkel, Barry D.
RJ506.S9A36   1989
362.2'8'0835 — dc20

                                              89-19773
                                               CIP

Adolescent Suicide: Recognition, Treatment and Prevention

CONTENTS

ABOUT THE EDITORS

Barry Garfinkel, MD, is Director of the Division of Child and Adolescent Psychiatry at the University of Minnesota. Previously, he was Director of Graduate and Undergraduate Medical Education in child psychiatry at Brown University, Providence, Rhode Island. His clinical and research interests are in the areas of depression and suicide in children and adolescents, anxiety disorders, and pharmacological research in children and adolescents with Attention Deficit Hyperactivity Disorder and school-based suicide prevention programs.

Gordon Northrup, MD, a child psychiatrict, is on the staff of the Berkshire Mental Health Center in Pittsfield, Massachusetts, and on the affiliate staff of Austen Riggs Center in Stockbridge. A former director of an AAPSC child guidance clinic, Dr. Northrup now provides consultation to residental treatment schools for emotionally disturbed children and youth. He has written articles and edited *Milieu Therapy* on residential treatment.

Adolescent Suicide: Recognition, Treatment and Prevention

Youth Suicide Risk Assessment: Process and Model

Wander de C. Braga, MD

SUMMARY. This paper describes a multidisciplinary process and a tool useful in assessing the degree of risk presented by suicidal children and adolescents, especially those receiving treatment in residential programs. Factors that contribute to suicide risk are organized in seven dimensions, each to be assessed separately by the professional team. Global risk determination is attained by integrating findings in all dimensions. A protocol is provided to guide the team in systematically gathering the relevant data needed to complete this process.

Prediction and prevention of youth suicide remain challenging tasks for mental health practitioners. Those working in residential settings are frequently called upon to assess risk in terms of potential lethality, since suicidal forms of behavior (suicide talk, threats, gestures and attempts) are rather common in this population. Within the past five to six years, the author has used a process and a tool he developed at his agency* to assess risk. The process, as described here, is adapted for usage within a 24-hour type of setting (residential, group home, hospital unit, etc.). The protocol (see Appendix), however, is designed for application to various settings, including residential.

Dr. Wander de C. Braga is a Board Certified Child Psychiatrist who functions as the Clinical Director for Campus Programs, Parsons Child and Family Center, 60 Academy Road, Albany, NY 12208. He is also Clinical Associate Professor and Assistant Director of Training for Child Psychiatry at the Department of Psychiatry of the Albany Medical College of Union University.

---

*Parsons Child and Family Center, Albany, New York.

1

THE PROCESS

The cornerstone of risk assessment is a multidisciplinary team meeting especially scheduled to review the clinical features of a case targeted. The goals of this meeting are (1) to arrive at a prediction concerning the degree of risk, and (2) to assure that an appropriate preventive intervention is planned and later implemented. Of course, for this meeting to occur, staff in general and especially line staff need to be sufficiently trained to recognize warning signals of suicide. In addition, a communication policy must exist so that prompt scheduling of such a meeting can occur. Prior to this meeting, a psychiatric interview and record review of the child or adolescent in question is arranged. The multidisciplinary team members (child care workers, nurses, teachers, psychiatrists, social workers and other therapists) to participate in this meeting are asked to re-familiarize themselves in advance with the history and clinical details of the youth in question. The actual team meeting is a modified clinical case review, now focused on the issue of suicide. This focusing is accomplished by using the protocol presented later.

The main advantage of conducting this process as a multidisciplinary team effort is that staff in close contact with patient and family have at their fingertips a wealth of information which is based on intimate and detailed knowledge of the case. Such details greatly facilitate the process of quickly arriving at judicious clinical judgments.

THE TOOL

The clinical tool here described is a protocol which was devised on the basis of a review of the pertinent literature plus the accumulated experience of the author. The following basic assumptions were used in its construction: (a) risk factors for youth suicide can be identified and, (b) the more loading of such factors in a given individual, the greater the risk. While appearing quantitative, this protocol truly invites qualitative thinking. In fact, it is assumed that final judgments can only be properly made by using integrative and dynamic thinking, both of which grow out of clinical knowledge and experience. It must be stated that in constructing this protocol, the author chose not to accept the typology sometimes quoted in the literature that divides suicidal youth into "true commiters" and "attempters," the latter by definition not at serious risk. Instead, it is assumed that there is a psychological continuum from the suicide attempters to the suicide completers (Barnes 1986, Perlstein 1986).

Risk factors are grouped into seven dimensions: *family history, individual history, intent or motivation to die, psychiatric status, current life situation, plan* and *behavioral patterns*. Each dimension is broken down into various components, each to be indicated in the protocol as present, absent or not applicable. For each component the protocol provides space for qualitative notes or else to record the degree of reliability of the information available, to record issues of intensity, frequency, etc. At the end of each dimension, the rater is asked to summarize findings by indicating the perceived degree of risk for that dimension in isolation. The person chairing the meeting (a clinician experienced in assessing suicidality) arrives at this decision by weighing the presence or absence of the various subcomponents and taking into consideration qualitative matters that come to be discussed in the team meeting. A four-point scale is used for this purpose: "no risk," "mild risk," "moderate risk," and "severe risk." This rating is repeated for each of the seven dimensions. As this is completed, final risk determination is made, now integrating the findings of all dimensions. This is a complex task. In the author's opinion there are no currently available statistical nor precise quantitative ways to accomplish it, at least not on the basis of the framework here used. Clinical experience remains the best guide.

Attention is called for the fact that an additional rating of "very severe and acute" is included in this final determination. This is to alert staff as to the need for immediate protective intervention. Additionally, space is available at the end of protocol for notes concerning dynamics, positive factors which may mitigate against suicide, short- and long-term therapeutic management implications, impact on the various modalities of treatment being used (individual, group, family), etc. Of course, provision of safety and protection of life are immediate concerns. In the author's agency, cases deemed to belong in the "very severe and acute" category are referred for hospitalization on an emergency basis. Cases in other categories may remain in the residential program pending coverage availability, the specifics of the phase of treatment, level of comfort of staff in dealing with case, etc. As to practical interventions, we have found it helpful to match the determined level of risk to a clear and operationally defined level of milieu supervision. For instance, children and adolescents deemed to belong in the "mild" category are placed on "intensified observation" status: "close observation" is used for those in the moderate risk category and "constant observation," essentially a 1:1 coverage at all times, for the severe ones. Each level of supervision is detailed in the agency's Manual of Policies and Procedures, so that new staff can become acquainted with them when first oriented to the job.

Re-evaluation of risk and interventions used need to be done at intervals. Intervention plans will need to change pending response of the child or adolescent, and levels of supervision may need to be discontinued, intensified, modified, etc. Usually this is decided upon during the regularly scheduled team meetings occurring bi-weekly in the units.

RISK FACTORS REVIEWED

This section provides the reader with the rationale for selection of items that comprise the protocol accompanying this paper. Essentially, an effort is made to capture those items that favor risk, as well as those that mitigate against it. The protocol begins with an identificatory section where age, sex, religion, race and family employment status are to be noted. These demographic factors are important in that studies point out the preponderance of males over females in completed suicides (approximately 3 to 1 ratio) as well as the inverse relation concerning the frequency of non-fatal attempts. The rate per 100,000 population per year clearly increases with age, peaking for the group 20-24 years. It has been observed that the rate of change in the percentages over the past decade and a half show alarming increases for all youth groups, especially for those in the 15 to 19 years of age. Suicide rates among whites continue to exceed those of other racial groups and this is true for both sexes (Frederick 1985). Parental unemployment appears to strongly correlate with suicide attempts (Garfinkel et al. 1982), and a strong religious affiliation is inversely correlated. It must be kept in mind, however, that assessment of religiosity needs to be done with caution. For instance, in New York City, Puerto Rican children are over represented in statistics for attempted suicide, even though they are predominantly Catholics (Gould 1985).

1. Family History

There is ample consensus in the research and clinical literature as to the importance of family factors as correlated to suicide and suicide attempt in children and adolescents. The history of loss of a parent by death was reported as far back as half a century ago by Zilboorg (1936) and subsequently it has been cited with regularity (Dorpat, Jackson and Ripley 1965; Temby 1961; Morrison and Collier 1969; Greer 1966; Connell 1972). Notwithstanding, Hendin (1972) cautions that the nature of the relationship prior to separation or loss, and the relationship with the remaining parent subsequently, are critical factors to be considered.

Loss of parent(s) by abandonment, separation, divorce or child placement is another important factor. It is conceivable that these factors are indicators of family dysfunction, family breakdown or disorganization. Thus, the experience of loss on the part of the child or adolescent is likely to be one among many other untoward events. In fact, Crook and Raskin (1975) point out that separation per se may not predispose the child toward suicide, but a loss that is the end result of severe family dysfunction ("family alienation") may do so. Several other authors have concurred (Connell 1972; Haider 1968; Haldane and Haider 1967; Tishler 1980; Toolan 1975; Tuckman and Youngman 1964; Winn and Halla 1966).

Suicidal behaviors in family members has long been cited in the literature as a predisposing factor. A mediating variable here may be an affective disorder ("Major Depression"), which is thought to be at least partially genetically determined. Of course, the learned experience of having a close relative use suicide as a solution for problems deemed unsolvable cannot be discounted (Bergstrand and Otto 1962; Paulson, Stone and Sposto 1978; Shafer 1974; Teicher and Jacobs 1966).

A history of chronic alcoholism and/or serious drug abuse in parents has also been accepted as a factor increasing risk for suicide in youth. It has been hypothesized that chronic alcoholism relates to the depressive spectrum of affective disorders. Moreover, chronic alcoholism may be instrumental in contributing to family dysfunction and disorganization, as it may favor unemployment, family violence, physical and sexual abuse and also low social economic status, all of which are factors increasing risk (Garfinkel et al. 1982; Milcinski 1974; Tishler, McHenry and Morgan 1980).

Other serious psychiatric illness in parents (major depression, schizophrenia and other psychoses) are thought to increase risk in the offspring either directly, via biological mechanism, or through disturbed interactions. In all likelihood both mechanisms are contributory (Otto 1972; Reich, Rise and Mullaney 1986; Schulsinger, Ketty, Rosenthal et al. 1979). Equally important is the history of persistent suicidal ideation on the part of a parent. In this instance, the suicidal act by the child or adolescent may represent an acting out of a parent's wish to die. The child's suicide attempt may truly be a distorted manifestation of his or her desire to save a parent (Pfeffer, Conte, Plutchik and Jerrett 1979; Pfeffer, Conte, Plutchik and Jerrett 1980).

Finally, the history of chronic parental indifference, rejection, hostility and lack of "mutual validation" is a most important factor. In this connection some authors have referred to the "expendable child syndrome" (Sabbath 1969), a condition where a parent may harbor a wish that the child be gone or be dead. Of course, such children and adolescents are more prone to self destruction (Brown 1985; Glasser 1965; McIntire and Ayle 1973; Schrut 1964).

2. Individual History

It can hardly be overemphasized that the youth who perceives himself as having chronic problems with the family, and alienated from it, is at higher risk for suicide. All of those factors reviewed previously (under family history) need now to be considered from the individual perspective of the child or adolescent. While the importance of this aspect has been clearly documented (Cantor 1972; Green 1968; Otto 1966; Paulson 1978; Teicher 1970), it is also relevant to emphasize that not all youth living in disorganized, unsupportive and multi-problem families are suicidal. Obviously other factors are also operative, this being the advantage of a multi-dimensional approach.

Depression, an effective disorder, has been singled out as a major etiologic factor in suicide. Depression is usually manifested by sadness, self-deprecatory ideas, low self-esteem, withdrawal, lack of social and peer relations and other symptoms and signs. Human relationships, especially intimate ones, are necessary for the sustenance of the healthy self. Depression, besides engendering hopelessness, taxes the adaptive and coping abilities of the individual (Bakwin 1973; Barter 1968; Brennan 1986; Henderson 1977; Stengel 1965), compromises individual and social relationships, and therefore increases risk.

More recently research evidence has surfaced confirming the clinical impression that a child's or adolescent's serious involvement with drugs and alcohol correlates with increased risk for suicide. It is possible that the involvement with substances of abuse may itself reflect the child's or adolescent's attempt to escape from intolerable life situations. In addition, these substances may elicit disinhibition which, manifested as impulsivity, further complicates already intolerable life situations. Of course, impulsive forms of behavior may also be translated into attempts at self destruction. From another angle, several authors have correlated substance abuse, especially alcoholism, with depression (Caine 1978; Dorpat and Ripley 1960; Schonfeld 1967; Trautman 1966).

Adolescents may not directly complain about depression or sadness. Yet, they may more easily complain of chronic boredom, lack of interest for activities and simply lack of "drive." These symptoms frequently alternate with temper tantrums, restlessness, defiance, acting out and "dare devil" type of activities (Barraclough, Bunch, Nelson et al. 1974). Again, these symptoms are important to be assessed because of the well known correlation between longstanding depression and suicidal behavior.

Another factor that correlates with suicidality is the finding of multiple hospitalizations in the individual history. This is perhaps a measurement of psychiatric morbidity and thus an indicator of serious emotional and mental disorders experienced by the young person. Furthermore, repeated hospitalizations may increase risk by adding trauma in the form of lost hope for normal life. Equally important is a history of a multiplicity of contacts with social agencies, which may reflect family and social breakdown. (Garfinkel et al. 1982; Hauton, Valente and Rink 1977). Also, multiple and/or chronic medical illnesses increase stress and handicap coping abilities, thereby increasing risk. In themselves such illnesses may reflect a psychogenic factor related to self-directed aggression, of which a suicide attempt is but a dramatic expression (Goldney 1981; Gould 1965).

It is crucial that in obtaining individual history, an accurate assessment of past gestures or attempts be obtained. Obviously the hypothesis is that previous attempts correlate positively with likelihood of a final lethal act (Gispert et al. 1987; Hauton et al. 1982).

From the nosological perspective, a history of major depression, psychosis and borderline personality disorder should be especially noted. While it is clear that suicide is not a symptom of any particular psychiatric condition, the literature nevertheless singles out the above categories as implicated in a significant number of child/adolescent suicide and serious suicide attempts. Yet, it must be remarked that children and adolescents need not be depressed nor severely psychiatrically ill for suicidal behavior of a serious nature to occur (Carlson and Cantwell 1982; Graff and Mallin 1967; Inamader, Lewis, Siomopoulos et al. 1982; Otto 1967; Pfeffer 1977; Seiden 1966; Toolan 1962).

Excessive striving for accomplishments and concomitant perception of failure have been cited as increasing risk. For instance, it is known that the suicide rate among students is higher than that of a comparable group of non students. Yet, the literature clearly underscores the fact that suicide among students is not related to academic pressure, poor grades or school failure per se (Sartore 1976). The crucial issue here appears to be the perceived self-failure, which may correlate to chronic depression, pathological narcissism, low self esteem, etc.

3. Assessment of Intent
("Motivation to Die")

Thoughts about suicide may be either communicated or withheld from others. It is generally accepted that when a young person has persistent conscious awareness of a desire to do self harm, this implies that the ambivalence about dying is now tipping on the side of an increased self destructive potential. Yet, careful assessment is needed because the communication of a desire to die has obvious "instrumental" or "manipulative" aspects. For this reason, the presence or absence of suicidal ideation requires careful scrutiny on the part of the clinician. This is more so when one considers the practitioner's frequent experience of interviewing a young person who has just made a very serious attempt but who totally denies a desire to die. In this instance it appears that denial, minimization and repression quickly became operative after the attempt and the youth convincingly believes that he or she no longer desires or is in danger of self harm. Thus, the clinical presentation is that of a rather bland, "removed" and unconcerned youth. In assessing this item, it is important that the clinician makes qualitative statements, especially as to whether or not the lack of affect is the result of active defenses unconsciously operating in the youth.

As stated before, the expression of hopelessness, having "nothing to live for," and feelings of worthlessness are characteristics of the depressive syndrome which is acknowledged as a contributor to risk (Hirschfelt and Blumenthal 1986; Marks and Haller 1977; Pfeffer 1985). Equally important, if not more so, is the expression of intense hostility, hatred and homicidal thoughts. Suicide, as a result of self-directed aggression, has been discussed in the literature since Freud's original formulations on the dynamics of depression. The experience of this author has consistently emphasized the importance of this factor. Its elucidation in the clinical interview and history-taking is a must (MacDonald 1967; Menninger 1956; Pfeffer et al. 1979; Sector 1967; Stengel 1965).

Younger children lack the cognitive equipment to understand the finality of death. They may see it as not permanent, as a sleep state, or something temporary and perhaps even pleasant. Thus, it is possible for young children to succeed in committing suicide because they are measuring the value of their lives with an inadequate yardstick. Some authors have reported that even older adolescents may cling to the notion of reversibility of death (von Hug-Hellmath 1965; McIntire, Ayle and Strumpler 1972; Nagy 1959; Pfeffer et al. 1979). Also, one must keep in mind that the child's cognitive understanding of death fluctuates with affective states and levels of stress.

A child's expressed wish for reunion with a dead loved one is an example of the type of pleasant death fantasy. The person acutely grieving the loss of a loved object may see death as a way to attain a blissful state of reunion, thereby relieving currently experienced grief, deprivations and frustrations. Of course, in this situation one is to assess the availability or lack of emotional supports from the existing significant others. The nature of the relationship of the child with the lost parent prior to the loss is equally important, as well as the manner of the parent's death. Qualitative statements are helpful in assessing this item.

Manipulation and/or the wish to punish someone by one's own death is a complex issue to ascertain. Generally they are regarded as factors mitigating against risk. However, this should not be used to dismiss or minimize the seriousness of a threat or attempt, because they invariably are expressions of complex forces in the intrapsychic and environmental fields, usually betraying acute emotional distress. While the suicidal attempt may be a message that something is wrong, or a form of coercion or punishment, it also reflects intense personal distress and/or intolerable socio-familial stress (Acherby 1967; Jacobs 1971; Toolan 1975).

4. Psychiatric Status

This section in the protocol is generally filled out by a psychiatrist but other clinicians may as well do so depending on experience and familiarity with the issues involved. Most are self-explanatory but a few comments are in order.

A current diagnosis of affective disorder (especially depression), psychosis or borderline personality are factors that increase suicidal risk, and previously mentioned references are relevant here. The positive correlation between intense aggression, murderous impulses and unconscious hostility and impulsivity to suicidal risk has also been pointed out earlier. In the clinical interview some of these features are frequently indirectly expressed in dreams, fantasies, drawings, favorite hobbies, etc. Therefore, it is important for the practitioner to actively elicit such material in the interview preceding the suicidal risk determination. It is also assumed that repetitive dreams featuring death of self or others may betray an unconscious preoccupation with the desire to die.

Those patients presenting a defective reality testing may experience hallucinations directing them to kill themselves. This population is at a very high risk for suicide and the seriousness of such symptoms cannot be overemphasized. Of course, such material should be actively pursued during the preliminary clinical/psychiatric interview (Winn and Halla 1966).

Current psychiatric status also should clarify whether or not abuse of alcohol or drugs is the case. Previously mentioned references do apply here.

5. Current Life Situation ("Precipitating Factors")

In studying the sequence of life events leading to suicidal behavior, the work of Teicher (1970) and Jacobs (1971) has indicated that there are stages preceding a suicidal attempt: a long previous history of problems, an escalation of these problems in adolescence and a final stage of dissolving meaningful relationships leading to isolation and alienation which immediately precedes the actual attempt. In this regard the breakdown of a current love relationship ("teen romance") is an important factor to be kept in mind. Not uncommonly vulnerable adolescents cling desperately to one single intense relationship which, upon failing, precipitates deep disappointment, depression and suicidal behavior (Otto 1972).

Social isolation and alienation as precipitants of suicidal behavior have already been mentioned previously (under Individual History) and again it must be assessed in terms of current life experiences. Previously mentioned references do apply here and, additionally, see Miller (1975). The lack of support systems, or unavailability of somebody to turn to (a "life line" as it were), certainly increases risk for the young person in extreme distress.

It is not unusual for youth in residential treatment to commit crimes and face imprisonment. Prison means social rejection, loss of significant others, loneliness and an extremely stressful environment. An already vulnerable adolescent may go from panic to hopelessness under such circumstances and make a serious suicidal attempt (Johnson 1978). Equally important is the issue of teenage pregnancy. Increased distress, the possibility of social alienation and guilt affecting an already vulnerable girl clearly augment suicidal risk. The literature indicates that risk appears to be higher in single catholic girls and in those not coming from poverty areas (Gabrielson et al. 1970; Mattson et al. 1969).

Other stresses attendant to current treatment situations such as loss of therapist, absence of significant others through vacations or other interruptions of treatment, turn over and loss of favorite staff etc., are stresses that children and adolescents in placement frequently experience. Such losses may rekindle old unresolved losses and precipitate suicidal behavior.

6. Plan

A self-destructive plan that is rather specific as to time, place and mechanical details (method to carry it out) increases risk in that it betrays the amount of psychological energy involved in its elaboration and the strength of motivation to see it completed. Of course, details that make rescue difficult or impossible would further increase seriousness of risk. Availability of method and its accessibility are also important details to be looked at. Whether the child or adolescent is planning to use drugs, hanging, jumping from high places, cutting self, stabbing, using fire arms, or running in front of vehicles, it is important to assess the degree of availability and accessibility of such methods. The assessment of the potential lethality of the method considered is quite relevant here. While the method considered by the child may not be in reality lethal (i.e., wrist cutting) the youth in question may not realize it, while truly being intent on dying. Drugs are generally not immediately lethal and allow room for rescue, but they are the most used method in suicidal attempts (Begstrand and Otto 1962; Eisenberg 1980; Garfinkel and Golombex 1974; Mattson et al. 1969). In completed suicides, the ranking of the various methods used for youth 24 years of age and under is as follows: firearms and explosives; hanging and strangulation; poisoning by solid or liquid substances; poisoning by gasses, (especially carbon monoxide); other specified drugs; jumping from high places; barbiturates. A case is made that completed suicide by using prescription drugs is actually low in ranking (Frederich 1985).

7. Behavioral Patterns

Behavior has communicative value and it is important to assess certain aspects of it to infer suicidal risk. For instance, the child or adolescent who is frequently involved in accidents, self-injuries and "near misses" may be attempting to communicate inner preoccupation with his own death. This form of action language betrays fantasies involving "brushes with death" which themselves are the result of the intrapsychic interplay of impulses towards, and defenses against, self death. Additionally, preoccupation with death may surface in notes, compositions in school, and letters expressing a vague desire to die. However, if a clear suicidal note is present, of course risk is increased, since action of a specific type has already occurred in the process of writing it. Separating the manipulative aspects of such messages from the seriously lethal ones may not be easy. Yet, one must be reminded that several studies of completed suicides used notes left by the individual to reconstruct the motivational aspect of the suicide (Jacobs 1971).

Change in usual behavior patterns is important in that they may be manifestations of hopelessness, depression and withdrawal from the environment. Thus, one must consider as increasing risk the fact that an adolescent who regularly attended school now refuses to attend; that a good student experiences a progressive drop in academic grades; that a pro-social child is recently refusing to meet and go out with his or her friends.

The giving away of prized possessions is rather serious in that it is a form of saying good bye to loved ones. Even if there is a hope that the message will be received and help made available, such actions must be regarded as "leaving a will," thus placing the child at greater risk.

SOME PRACTICAL CONCLUDING REMARKS

The process of conducting a special team meeting and using the attached protocol to assess risk for suicide results in the accumulation of a great deal of data that needs interpretation. Experienced clinicians are able to do that while being aware that predictions shall remain tentative. It is crucial that a well structured process be mobilized and accomplished, not only to satisfy legal and accountability demands, but mostly to generate plans and activities that protect life. This is time consuming, creating logistical problems for hardpressed staff. Furthermore, it is well known that the number of suicide attempts far outstrip the number of completed ones (statistics range from 50 to 1 to 300 to 1). The dilemma for clinicians is to separate the serious ones from those that are not so. In a residential program, where the level of psychopathology is likely to be high, it would not be prudent to take a "laissez-faire" attitude towards suicidal behavior. Yet, the number of such behaviors may be so high that it is totally impossible to mobilize this complex process every time a youth makes a suicidal verbalization or gesture. A "triage" is necessary and the author reserves this process for the following conditions:

— for a new resident, not yet well known by staff, who comes in with a complaint of past serious suicidal behavior;
— repetitive suicidal communication and behaviors that do not respond as expected in the usual treatment program;
— unpredicted, unsuspected serious gesture.

The mobilization of this more elaborate assessment as a "post facto" process is a limitation that could only be avoided by its routine application to all youth in programs, a logistical impossibility and perhaps an unwise clinical decision.

The reader is also cautioned as to the practical difficulty in using this provided protocol. Items are not ranked, discussions are heterogenous and, frequently, precise data for certain items is not available or is unclear. This means the protocol is at best seen as a clinical guideline to remind clinicians as to the important areas that need review, so that judicious conclusions can be reached. In addition, the protocol as presented applies to various settings. Those items that are not relevant for youth in a residential program should be indicated as such in the "not applicable" column.

The author's experience in using this process and tool in residential populations indicates that there are two profiles that by themselves elevate risk at least to the severe level. First, is the adolescent with a past history of several losses, multiple placements, lack of a sense of belonging in a nuclear family, who is filled with anger and hatred and who may entertain fantasies of future revenge against significant others. Such an adolescent usually mobilizes attention and concern from treatment figures because of their aggressivity, impulsivity and potential for violence. It is easy to forget that they may become seriously suicidal if they lose connectedness with the treatment setting, for instance, in the aftermath of a precipitous discharge. The second profile that requires immediate protective action is that of the psychotic child or adolescent entertaining hallucinatory experiences ("voices") commanding them to kill themselves. These youth perceive themselves as filled with "badness," and suicide may be their irrational way of protecting those in the milieu they care about.

REFERENCES

Acherby, W.C. Latency-age children who threaten or attempt to kill themselves. *Journal of the American Academy of Child Psychiatry*, 6, 242-261, 1967.

Bakwin, R.M. Suicide in children and adolescents. *Journal of the American Medical Women's Association*, 18(12), 643-650, 1973.

Barnes, R.A. The recurrent self-harm patient. *Suicide and Life Threatening Behavior*, 16(4), 1986.

Barraclough, B.; Bunch, J.; Nelson, B. et al. A hundred cases of suicide: Clinical aspects. *British Journal of Psychiatry*, 125, 355-373, 1974.

Barter, J.T. et al. Adolescent suicide attempts. *Archives of General Psychiatry*, 19, 523-527, 1968.

Bergstrand, C.G. and Otto, U. Suicidal attempts in adolescence and childhood. *Acta Paediatrica Scandinavica*, 50, 17-26, 1962.

Brennan, T. Adolescent loneliness: Linking epidemiology and theory to prevention. In G. Klerman (Ed.), *Suicide and depression among adolescents and young adults*, Washington, D.C.: American Psychiatric Press, Inc., 1986.

Brown, S.L. Adolescents and family systems, In M.L. Peck, N.L. Garberow and R.E. Litman (Eds.), *Youth suicide*. New York: Springer Publishing Co., 1985.

Caine, E. Two contemporary tragedies: Adolescent suicide/adolescent alcoholism. *National Association Private Psychiatric Hospitals*, 9(3), 4-11, 1978.

Cantor, P. The adolescent attempter: Sex, sibling position and family constellation. *Life-Threatening Behavior*, 2(4), 252-261, 1972.

Carlson, G.A. and Cantwell, D.P. Suicidal behavior and depression in children and adolescents. *Journal of the American Academy of Child Psychiatry*, 21(4), 361-368, 1982.

Connell, H.M. Attempted suicide in school children. *Medical Journal of Australia*, 1, 686-690, 1972.

Crook, T. and Raskin, A. Association of childhood parental loss with attempted suicide and depression. *Journal of Consulting and Clinical Psychologists*, 43(2), 227, 1975.

Dorpat, T.L. and Ripley, H.S. A study of suicide in the Seattle area. *Comprehensive Psychiatry*, 1, 347-359, 1960.

Dorpat, T.L.; Jackson, J. and Ripley, H. Broken homes and attempted and completed suicides. *Archives of Genetic Psychiatry*, 12(2), 213-216, 1965.

Eisenberg, L. Adolescent suicide: On taking arms against a sea of troubles. *Pediatrics*, 315-320, 1980.

Frederick, C.J. An introduction and overview of youth suicide. In M.L. Peck; N.L. Farberow and R.E. Litman (Eds.), *Youth suicide*. New York: Springer Publishing Co., 1985.

Gabrielson, I.W. et al. Suicide attempts in a population pregnant as teenagers. *American Journal of Public Health*, 60, 2289-2301, 1970.

Garfinkel, B.D. and Golombex, K. Suicide and depression in childhood and adolescence. *Canadian Medical Association Journal*, 110, 1278-1281, 1974.

Garfinkel, B.D. et al. Suicide attempts in children and adolescents. *American Journal of Psychiatry*, 139(10), 1257-1261, October 1982.

Gispert, M. et al. Predictive factors in repeated suicide attempts by adolescents. *Hospital and Community Psychiatric*, 38(4), 390-393, 1987.

Glaser, K. Attempted suicide in children and adolescents: Psychodynamic observations. *American Journal of Psychotherapy*, 19, 220-227, 1965.

Goldney, R.D. Attempted suicide in young females; correlates of lethality. *British Journal of Psychiatry*, 139, 382-390, 1981.

Gould, R.E. Suicide problems in children and adolescents. *American Journal of Psychotherapy*, 19, 228-246, 1965.

Graff, H. and Mallin, R. The syndrome of the wrist cutter. *American Journal of Psychiatry*, 124, 36-42, 1967.

Green, A.H. Self-destructive behavior in battered children. *American Journal of Psychiatry*, 133(5), 578-582, 1968.

Greer, S. Parental loss and attempted suicide: A further report. *British Journal of Psychiatry*, 112, 465-470, 1966.

Haider, I. Suicidal attempts in children and adolescents. *British Journal of Psychiatry*, 114, 1133-1134, 1968.

Haldane, J.D. and Haider, I. Attempted suicide in children and adolescents, *British Journal of Clinical Practice*, 21(12), 587-591, 1967.

Halton, C.L.; Valente, S. and Rink, A. *Suicide: Assessment and intervention*. New York: Appleton-Century-Crofts, 1977.

Hauton, K. et al. Adolescents who take overdoses: Their characteristics, problems, and contacts with helping agencies. *British Journal of Psychiatry*, 140, 118-123, 1982.

Henderson, A.S. et al. A typology of parasuicide. *British Journal of Psychiatry*, 131, 631-641, 1977.

Hendin, H. Suicide among the young: Psychodynamics and demography. In M.L. Peck; N.L. Farberow and R.E. Litman, *Youth suicide*. New York, Springer Publishing Co., 1985.

Hirschfeld, R.M. and Blumenthal, S.J. Personality, life event, and other psychosocial factors in adolescent depression and suicide. In G. Klerman (Ed.), *Suicide and depression among adolescents and young adults*, Washington, D.C., American Psychiatric Press, Inc., 1986.

Inamader, S.; Lewis, D.; Siomopoulos, G. et al. Violent and suicidal behavior in psychotic adolescents. *American Journal of Psychiatry*, 139, 932-935, 1982.

Jacobs, J. *Adolescent suicide*. New York: Wiley-Interscience, 1971.

Johnson, R.J. Youth in crisis: Discussions of self-destructive conduct among adolescent prisoners. *Adolescence*, 13(51), 461-482, 1978.

MacDonald, J.M. Homicidal threats. *American Journal of Psychiatry*, 124, 475-482, 1967.

Marks, P.A. and Haller, D.L. Now I lay me down for keeps: A study of adolescent suicide attempts. *Journal of Clinical Psychology*, 33, 390-400, 1977.

Mattson, A. et al. Suicidal behavior as a child psychiatry emergency: Clinical characteristics and follow-up results. *Archives of General Psychiatry*, 20, 100-109, 1969.

McIntire, M.S.; Ayle, C.R. and Strumpler, L.J. The concept of death in midwestern children and youth. *American Journal of Diseases of Children*, 123, 527-532, 1972.

McIntire, M.S. and Ayle, C.R. Psychological "biopsy" in self-poisoning of children and adolescents. *American Journal of Diseases of Children*, 126, 42-46, 1973.

Menninger, K. *Man against himself*. New York: Harcourt and Brace, 1956.

Milcinski, W. Parents of the juvenile who committed suicide in Slovenia. In N. Speyer et al. (Eds.), *Proceedings of the 7th international congress on suicide prevention*. Amsterdam: Swets and Zeitlinger, B.V., 1974.

Miller, J.P. Suicide and adolescence. *Adolescence*, 10(37), 11-24, 1975.

Morrison, G.C. and Collier, J.G. Family treatment approaches to suicidal children and adolescents. *Journal of the American Academy of Child Psychiatry*, 8, 140-153, 1969.

Nagy, M.H. The child's view of death. In H. Feifel (Ed.), *The meaning of death*. New York: McGraw-Hill, 1959.

Otto, V. Suicidal attempts made by children. *Acta Paediatrica Scandinavica*, 55, 64-72, 1966.

Otto, V. Suicidal attempts made by psychotic children and adolescents. *Acta Paediatrica Scandinavica*, 56, 349-356, 1967.

Otto, V. Suicidal acts by children and adolescents: A follow-up study. *Acta Psychiatrica Scandinavia*, 223 (supplement), 5-123, 1972.

Paulson, M.J.; Stone, D. and Sposto, R. Suicide behavior and behavior in children ages 4 to 12. *Suicide and Life Threatening Behavior*, 8(4), 225-242, 1978.

Perlstein, A.P. Suicide in adolescence. *New York State Journal of Medicine*, (23), 3017-3020, 1986.

Pfeffer, C.R. Psychiatric hospital treatment of suicidal children. *Suicidal and Life-Threatening Behavior*, 8(3), 150-160, 1977.

Pfeffer, C.R.; Conte, H.R.; Plutchik, R. and Jerrett, I. Suicidal behavior in latency-age children: An empirical study. *Journal of the American Academy of Child Psychiatry*, 18(4), 679-692, 1979.

Pfeffer, C.R.; Conte, H.R.; Plutchik, R. and Jerrett, I. Suicidal behavior in latency-age children: An outpatient population. *Journal of the American Academy of Child Psychiatry*, 19, 703-710, 1980.

Pfeffer, C.R. Observations of ego functioning of suicidal latency-age children. In M.L. Peck, N.L. Barberow and R.E. Litman (Eds.), *Youth suicide*. New York, Springer Publishing Co., 1985.

Reich, T.; Rice, J. and Mullaney, J. Genetic risk factors for the affective disorders. In G. Klerman (Ed.), *Suicide and depression among adolescents and young adults*. Washington, D.C.: American Psychiatric Press, Inc., 1986.

Sabbath, J.C. The suicidal adolescent—the expendable child. *Journal of the American Academy of Child Psychiatry*, 8, 272-285, 1969.

Sartore, R.L. Students and suicide: An interpersonal tragedy. *Theory into Practice*, 15(5), 337-339, 1976.

Schonfeld, W.A. Socioeconomic influence as a factor. *New York State Journal of Medicine*, 67(14), 1981-1990, 1967.

Schrut, A. Suicidal adolescents and children. *Journal of the American Medical Association*, 188(13), 1103-1197, 1964.

Schulsinger, F.; Ketty, S.S.; Rosenthal, D. et al. A family study of suicide. In M. Schou and E. Stromgren (Eds.), *Origin, prevention, and treatment of affective disorders*. London and New York: Academic Press, 1979.

Sector, D. Suicide as an aggressive act. *Journal of Psychology*, 66, 47-50, 1967.

Seiden, R.H. Campus tragedy: A study of student suicide. *Journal of Abnormal Psychology*, 7(6), 389-399, 1966.

Shaffer, D. Suicide in childhood and early adolescence. *Journal of Child Psychology and Psychiatry*, 15, 275-291, 1974.

Stengel, E. *Suicide and attempted suicide*. Bristol, England: MacGibbon and Kee, Ltd., 1965.

Teicher, J.D. and Jacobs, J. Adolescents who attempt suicide: Preliminary findings. *American Journal of Psychiatry*, 122(11), 1248-1257, 1966.

Teicher, J.D. Children and adolescents who attempt suicide. *Pediatric Clinics of North America*, 17(3), 687-696, 1970.

Temby, W.D. Suicide. In G. Blaine and C. McArthur (Eds.). *Emotional problems of the student*. New York: Appleton-Century-Crofts, 1961.

Tishler, C.L.; McHenry, P.C. and Morgan, K.C. Adolescent suicide attempts: Some significant factors. *Suicide and Life Threatening Behavior*, 11, 86-92, 1980.

Tishler, C.L. Intentional self-destructive behavior in children under age ten. *Clinical Pediatrics*, 19(7), 471-453, 1980.

Toolan, J.M. Suicide and suicide attempts in children and adolescents. *American Journal of Psychiatry*, 118(8), 719-724, 1962.

Toolan, J. Suicide and suicide attempts in children and adolescents. *American Journal of Psychotherapy*, 29, 339-344, 1975.

Trautman, E.C. Drug abuse and suicide attempts of an adolescent girl: A social and psychiatric evaluation. *Adolescence*, 1(4), 381-392, 1966.

Tuckman, J. and Youngman, W.F. Attempted suicide and family disorganization. *Journal of Genetic Psychology*, 105, 187-193, 1964.

von Hug-Hellmath, H. The child's concept of death. *Psychoanalytic Quarterly*, 34, 499-516, 1965.

Winn, D. and Halla, R. Observations of children who threaten to kill themselves. *Canadian Psychiatric Association Journal, II* (supplement), 283-294, 1966.

Zilboorg, G. Differential diagnostic types of suicide. *Archives of Neurology and Psychiatry*, 35, 270-291, 1936.

BIOGRAPHICAL NOTE

Dr. Braga, a native Brazilian, received his medical degree from the University of Saõ Paulo. In 1965 he began his residency training in general psychiatry at the Menninger School of Psychiatry in Topeka, Kansas. Following training he joined the staffs of the Kansas Reception and Diagnostic Center and the Topeka State Hospital, while teaching as an instructor at Menninger's psychiatric educational programs. In 1971, and still in Topeka, he started the career training in child psychiatry and upon its completion in 1973 he moved to Albany, New York. He is currently the Clinical Director of Campus Programs of Parsons Child and Family Center. On a part-time basis, he is on the staff of the Capital District Psychiatric Center, a teaching hospital associated with the Department of Psychiatry and Division of Child and Adolescent Psychiatry of the Albany Medical College.

In 1973 Dr. Braga was honored with the Elmer E. Southard Award for Medical Writing given by the Children's Division of the Menninger Clinic; twice since he has been honored with the Distinguished Teacher of Psychiatry Award given by the Department of Psychiatry of the Albany Medical College.

He is married and has three children. For fun he likes carpentry, playing the classical guitar, listening to music and fishing.

APPENDIX A
Family History

a. loss of parent(s) by death (note if by suicide)

b. loss of parent(s) by abandonment, separation, divorce, placements, etc.

c. history of suicide among closer relatives

d. alcoholism and/or serious drug abuse in parents

e. history of serious psychiatric illness in parents. Note if chronic depression and psychiatric hospitalization have occurred

f. history of persistent suicidal ideation in parent(s)

g. history of parental indifference, rejection, hostility

_____ Number of Risk Factors

Individual History

a. history of chronic problems with, and alienation from, the family
b. loneliness, withdrawal, lack of social/peer relations
c. serious involvement with alcohol/drugs
d. chronic boredom, lack of interest for activities
e. past psychiatric hospitalizations and social agencies contacts
f. history of multiple and/or chronic medical illnesses
g. past suicidal gestures, attempts (note methods used)
h. past diagnosis of major depression, or psychosis, or borderline personality
i. history of excessive strivings for accomplishments and experiences of "failure(s)"

_____ Number of Risk Factors

Intent ("Motivation to die")

a. subject consciously acknowledges and expresses wishes to die (suicidal ideation)
b. expresses hopelessness and feelings that "there is nothing to live for," worthlessness
c. expresses intense hostility, hatred, homicidal thoughts
d. death is seen as "sleep," "temporary" and reversible, "pleasant"
e. expresses wishes of reunion with dead loved one
f. "manipulation" and wish to punish someone by own death

_____ Number of Risk Factors

Current Psychiatric Status

a. current diagnosis of affective disorder
b. diagnosis of borderline personality or psychosis
c. unconscious hostility, murderous impulses
d. dreams featuring death, self or others
e. poor concentration, loss of appetite, loss of weight, "psychosomatic" complaints
f. presence of psychotic symptoms, especially self-directed destructive ideation
g. current abuse of alcohol/drugs

_____ Number of Risk Factors

Life Situation

a. long-standing history of environmental/familial "problems" which more recently have escalated
b. breakdown of current love relationship (teen romance)
c. social isolation/alienation, lack of interest for social relationships
d. nobody to turn to, lack of "support systems"
e. imprisonment
f. teenage pregnancy
g. stress in current treatment

_____ Number of Risk Factors

Plan

a. plan is very specific in terms of method, time, place, details, etc.
b. method thought about is available and accessible
c. method of accomplishing suicide is highly lethal

_____ Number of Risk Factors

Important Behavioral Patterns

a. frequent accidents, injuries, "near misses" more recently
b. has left letters, notes, etc. expressing wish to die
c. there is a suicidal note
d. sudden change of patterns: school refusal, grades are dropping, doesn't want to see friends, etc.
e. seems to be leaving a "will" (i.e., giving away prized possessions, etc.)

_____ Number of Risk Factors

Summary of Behavioral Pattern:

Residential Management
of Suicidal Adolescents

Andrew Edmund Slaby, PhD, MD, MPH
Patricia L. McGuire, MD

> "These graves are all too young,
>   From the world's bitter wine
>   Seek shelter in the shadow of the tomb"
>
> *Percy Byssch Shelley*

Mortality rates in early and mid-life have declined remarkably over the past century with the exception of those aged 15-24 in the past two decades. In this group, rates have increased from 106 to 119 per 100,000.[1] Violent deaths: suicide, homicide and accidents account for the increase. Depression is a risk factor not limited to suicide. Depressed youths drink or take drugs and drive. Decreased reaction time and careless driving can contribute to their own injury or death and that of innocent others. Forty-five to 50% of fatal car crashes in this group are associated with alcohol use.[2] Depression in the young often presents as instability and anger.[3] Anger leads to fighting. Fighting, to death.

Suicide rate per 100,000 in the group 15 to 24 has increased nearly 250% from 6.8 to 17.4 over 20 years with the rate not achieved again until 55.[4] Increase is greatest among males—three times that of females. Experts estimate true figures for completed

Andrew Edmund Slaby is Medical Director, Fair Oaks Hospital, Summit, NJ, Psychiatrist-in-Chief, The Regent Hospital, New York, NY, Clinical Professor of Psychiatry, New York University, New York, NY, Adjunct Clinical Professor of Psychiatry, New York Medical College, New York, NY, Adjunct Professor of Psychiatry and Human Behavior, Brown University, Providence, RI. Patricia L. McGuire is Attending Psychiatrist, Fair Oaks Hospital, Summit, NJ.

suicides to be three times reported rates.[4] Taboos, impact on relatives, and exclusionary clauses in insurance policies militate against more accurate disclosure. While actual suicide among children is rare (although perhaps deceivingly so because children who walk in front of cars are reported as traffic deaths and not as suicide if intent is not known), suicidal behavior is common.[3,5,6] As many as 10% of inpatient and outpatient children being seen for psychiatric problems have exhibited suicidal behavior and as many as 72% of child psychiatric inpatients have entertained the idea of suicide.[7]

CLINICAL PRESENTATION

Evaluation and management of adolescent suicide presents unique problems. The young are not as facile in ability to identify symptoms and signs of depression. Symptoms, in addition, differ.[8-10] Sleep and appetite may or may not be impaired. Failing grades, truancy, drug and alcohol use, social withdrawal, and accidents may be the only indications. Depressed children may walk in front of an oncoming train or car or suffer multiple athletic injuries.

Youth's concept of death differs from that of adults. Some investigators have failed to link youth suicide with a particular concept of death, while others find suicidal children perceive death as transient and pleasant.[8,12,13] Most suicidal children are preoccupied with thoughts of death and dying.[14] There is obviously reason to believe that finality of death is incomprehensible to latency age children and conceived of only on an impersonal level by adolescents, unless they have experienced a sibling's or friend's premature death. Factors contributing to adolescent suicide include a cry for help, desire to join a lost one, desire to vanish, desire to escape, guilt, anger, and evolving psychosis.[6,8,15,16] A critical factor in the perceived lower suicide rates of children may be the lack of social isolation, a variable seen as key to adult suicide. Children, given their helpless status, are enveloped with rare exception with at least nominal support for food, clothing and shelter. They enter adolescence, they become more adult. Adults withdraw from adolescents and sometimes demean them. Peers pressure youths sexually and chemically with drugs and alcohol. Adolescents are pressured by parents to achieve and, ironically, when adolescents excel, their peers pressure them to be more normal.

Substance abusing adolescents are often more depressed. Depression may be self-medicated by drugs and as inability to resist alcohol or drug use leads to depression. In cases of amphetamine and cocaine use, depression precedes drug use.[16-18] In either instance, research indicates nontransitory depression often exists in concert with major depressive disorder (so-called "double depression").[17] Double depression in some can lead to increased physical symptoms as a barometer of psychic pain; in others, to suicide attempts or successes.

Plasticity of the evolving adolescent personality creates a number of problems for psychiatric clinicians treating this age group but also affords opportunities for intervention that do not exist at other stages of development. Both real change and development of coping styles may occur.[19-25] To achieve growth, a strategy to effect change must be defined that commences with early identification and concludes with maximization of post-hospital care. Characterologic and economic forces limit choices, but if efforts are made to achieve the best in care, permanent change is possible.

RISK FACTORS

Continued evaluation of risk for suicide is imperative at each stage of care to provide timely intervention to prevent death and enduring patterns of self-destructive behavior.[26-29] Characteristics of completers differ from repeater attempters.[12,13,15] While most who succeed have attempted, only a fraction of those who attempt, succeed. Description of adolescent suicides and attempters and contributing factors are portrayed in Tables 1 and 2.

Adolescents most likely to die by suicide have *treatable* psychiatric illness: bipolar disorder, major depression, or schizophrenia. They are less likely to be characterologically disturbed than multiple abortive attempters. Good students and student leaders die by suicide. Sometimes they were good students and good leaders because they had double depression. They had dysthymic disorder and then got major depression. Mild chronic depression characteristic of dysthymic disorder caused them to listen more and be more respon-

TABLE 1
CHARACTERISTIC OF SUICIDES AND PARASUICIDES

COMPLETERS	ATTEMPTERS
Are more frequently male	Are more frequently female
Have more major psychiatric disorders (e.g. depression, schizophrenia)	Have more character disorders (e.g. borderline and antisocial personalities)
Gave warning in previous years	
Have more family histories of mental illness	Are more frequently Protestant
Made previous attempts in secret	
Are more intelligent	Perform more poorly academically
Had more frequently experienced suicide in a family member or peer	Have more obvious problems with with parents, peers, and siblings
Used more lethal measures (e.g., guns, hanging, jumping) in previous attempts	Are more public about attempts
Had fewer obvious problems with parents, siblings, and peers	Tend to use less lethal means (e.g., overdose)
Had made previous suicide attempts	
Were successful at school	Make attempts impulsively
Felt Hopelessness	
Used more alcohol and drugs	
Felt worthlessness	Use less lethal measures
Were preoccupied with death	
Had more social isolation, withdrawal, and lack of communication	
Wished to die	
Believed more that death is pleasant and temporary	
Experienced more abuse at home	
Experience more perinatal distress	

TABLE 2

STRESSORS

ENVIRONMENTAL	INDIVIDUAL
Academic failure	Acute or chronic illness
Breakup of love affair	Delinquency
Child rearing practices	Desire to be united with some dead
Communication problems	Existential nihilism
Crowding	Feeling unwanted
Cultural sanctions	Guilt
Disintegration of social supports	Impulsivity
Family problems	Loneliness
Loss of parent through death, divorce or separation	Perinatal distress
Models of suicide	Revenge
Overt sexual encounters	Secondary gain
Peer rejection	Sexual confusion
Physical and sexual abuse	
Unemployment	

sive to other needs contributing both to a conveyed image of "sensitivity" and to an aura of being "responsive and responsible." Childhood depression, introjection as a defense, parental suicidal tendencies, and belief in an afterlife are greater for suicidal than nonsuicidal children.[23] More normal nonsuicidal aggressive children see death as final.

School performance relates to predominant diagnosis. If a child is characterologically disturbed, as are many of repeaters, one expects to see intermittent or protracted periods of poor performance. When an attempt results from major psychiatric illness, decline in school performance parallels the increasing intensity of the illness.

Youth suicides predominate in late afternoon and parallel seasonal fluctuations seen with that of adults with greater numbers in Spring.[30]

Major psychiatric illness, hopelessness, and lack of social support are probably the three most critical variables impacting on desire to die. Even when suicide occurs with complex partial seizures or as a side effect of antihypertensive medication victims feel hopeless. Children, like adults when depressed, perceive parents differently than when euthymic. Irritability and acting out in an attempt to control when depression makes one feel out of control contributes to development of losses and low self-esteem which may be mistakenly perceived as etiological rather than symptomatic. Depressed adolescents feel hopeless. Depressed parents beget depressed children both genetically and by serving as models for identification and for maladaptive coping styles, i.e., "learned helplessness." Depressed adolescents withdraw to hide depression. Irritability leads to others leaving them. Depressed children feel they are to be blamed for domestic turmoil and perceive themselves as unwanted.[22,31-33] (See Table 3.)

A major source of confusion in the literature has been failure to distinguish suicidal children (which includes repeaters and completers) from those at greatest risk which can only be extrapolated from study of the population of completers.[3,4,12,13,15,18,34] Comparison of repeaters and completers affords understanding of where to focus limited health resources such as intensive inpatient treatment and residential care. This does not minimize the need for managing repeaters. Most who succeed have attempted and attempts may lead inadvertently to death, prolonged physical morbidity (brain damage, paraplegia), and enduring maladaptive functioning. One of the most striking differences between suicidal children and similarly aged, psychiatrically ill, nonsuicidal children is degree of violence (as high as 66%) in families of suicidal children.[7] Suicide attempts are one of the sequelae of child abuse.

It is clear from a review of factors surrounding child and adolescent suicide attempts—parental discord or separation, physical or sexual abuse, parental substance abuse, major psychiatric illness in parents, and lack of social supports—that a significant number of suicidal adolescents will benefit from more extended structured care

TABLE 3

INDICANTS OF ADOLESCENT SUICIDAL INTENT

- Accidents
- Aggression
- Depression
- Excessive guilt
- Giving away prized possessions
- Helplessness
- Hopelessness
- Hypersensitivity
- Impulsivity
- Isolation
- Low frustration tolerance
- Low self-esteem
- Poor school performance
- Psychomotor retardation
- Risk-taking behavior
- Sadness
- Sleep disturbance
- Substance abuse
- Suicidal ideation
- Unusual neglect of appearance
- Withdrawal
- Worthlessness

than a hospital with limited stay or an outpatient clinic can provide. This is the role of residential care where children find social support, sanctuary from physical or sexual abuse, opportunity to learn new ways of coping with dysphoric affect, protection from substance abusing peers, and reprieve from conflict between parents.

RESIDENTIAL MANAGEMENT

Preacceptance Assessment

It is necessary to determine the degree of acute suicidal ideation or intent as well as evolving or episodic physical illness (complex partial seizures) that contributes to self destructive behavior before assuming residential responsibility for a self-destructive child or adolescent. Suicidal adolescents present for residential care after having failed to master developmental tasks characteristic of their age and after having failed to end their struggle through suicide. They are often unwilling to participate in treatment and are antagonistic to providing information required for assessment, diagnosis, and development of a treatment plan. A multidisciplinary approach is best to evaluate a child's family in its milieu and the extended social system (via school church, and community components).

The highest priority in evaluating suicidal adolescents for residential care is safety. If the patient is not referred from a hospital, a medical history is obtained, physical exam performed, and indicated laboratory and psychological tests performed. Staff have to create an environment to meet a standard of safety to prevent further self-destruction if it is not readily available. In such instances, a staff member may need to be in constant attendance to insure sufficient time for evaluation and acute management. If admission to a general hospital as opposed to residential setting is indicated, the same standard of safety must be extended to the inpatient unit. This may require continued constant observation. Regardless of level of staffing, an environment where acutely ill adolescents are treated should be secure; cords and hangers removed, dinnerware and plates constructed of plastic or cardboard; and windows provided that cannot be opened too far or broken.

Psychiatric Consultation

Psychiatric consultants are not always welcomed by adolescents but a nonjudgmental empathetic approach gains cooperation. Potential lethality of a suicide attempt is assessed from history. Method used is important. Attempt by gun or hanging is statistically more likely to have resulted in death than drug overdose. Risk is associated with likelihood of discovery. Attempters in isolated cabins in a forest are less likely to be discovered than adolescents who attempt in a bathroom or bedroom and leave the door open and an empty pill box on the floor. On the whole, planned considered attempts are potentially more lethal than those performed impulsively. Some youngsters impulsively overdose with cyanide and do not think of the fact that death rapidly ensues. Previous suicide attempts and sustained mood disorder enhance risk of future attempts. (See Table 4.)

Denial has no place in the evaluation of adolescents. Skillful interviewing and a high index of suspicion are required to document the nature and degree of suicidal intent. Suspicion warrants referral for reevaluation and treatment in another setting if required. Adolescents may be embarrassed by feelings of turmoil that resulted in a self-destructive act. Attention of mental health professionals may humiliate them despite obvious need for help. They may, as a result, hesitate to share their thoughts and obfuscate pain through projected hostility. A consistent, empathetic, nonjudgmental approach allows a patient to self-disclose and reveal thoughts and feelings. Despite overt resistance, an adolescent often feels over-

TABLE 4

ELEMENTS IN INITIAL ASSESSMENT

Nature and circumstances leading up to and including the suicide attempt

Relative risk for recurrence

History of affective and/or psychotic disorder

Alcohol and drug use history

Family history of psychiatric illness

Intrafamilial relationships

Developmental history

Medical history

Friendship network

Extrafamilial activities

School performance

Work history

Previous self-destructive behavior

whelmed and out of control because of conflicting and self-destructive feelings. A great sense of relief results from being placed in a controlled environment that prohibits acting out suicidal impulses.

Danger of recurrence is assessed at initial interview and periodically during hospitalization and subsequent residential treatment. Pressure to act on suicidal thoughts and desire to prevent self from acting on the pressure is monitored. The existence of a specific plan to act and availability of means to execute plan (cord to hang self, nonsecured window) concurrent with a sense of hopelessness for the future is a dangerous combination. Sarcastic remarks should be construed as serious threats. Inconsistencies in speech, behavior, and affect should be carefully evaluated.

> A 13 year old patient with anorexia nervosa complicated by bingeing and vomiting was anticipating discharge following prolonged inpatient hospitalization. She returned from a weekend pass with renewed suicidal ideation. Prior to leaving for a pass the next day, a psychiatrist discussed the suicidal thoughts she was expressing. She states: "Oh, I always feel that way. The problem is I don't act on it. Besides, my Dad wouldn't let anything happen." Her pass was revoked that day and her depressive symptoms were reevaluated and treated.

A differential diagnosis that includes major and minor psychiatric disorders and concurrent character and medical disorders is developed from history, mental status, physical exam, and ancillary clinical tests. Central to a successful treatment plan is recognition of pharmacologically responsive illnesses that first present in adolescence, such as major depression or paranoid schizophrenia. The preponderance of adolescent suicide represents undiagnosed affective illness. Other diagnoses, however, must be considered. Patients experiencing command hallucinations during a brief psychotic episode may carry out the order to commit suicide. Reactive disturbances reflecting a transient psychological response to environmental stresses rather than an endogenous process are also found in the population of suicidal adolescents.[35-58]

Alcohol and drug use contribute to impulsivity leading to covert or overt acting out of suicidal impulses. Substance abuse mimics psychiatric disturbances (amphetamine-induced paranoia, alcohol-induced depression, PCP-induced affective states) as well as precipitates dormant psychoses. Drugs and alcohol disinhibit previously stable adolescents impairing judgement and producing dysphoria resulting in acting out self-injurious behavior (driving cars at high speeds, running across interstate highways, hitchhiking under compromised disturbances). Substance abuse history broadens differential diagnosis and provides keys to the etiology of suicidal ideation. A comprehensive drug screen is part of the initial evaluation and complements clinical evidence of delirium, instability of vital signs, and nature of psychiatric symptoms.

Family Assessment

A family may be in acute crisis following an unexpected suicide attempt. Guilt, anger, and frustration prevents parents and siblings from providing the details of the adolescents' problems as they perceive them. Support provided by therapists facilitates obtaining historical data as families recover from the initial shock and begin to explore the dimensions of the problem. A sympathetic approach to needs and concerns of the family produces a therapeutic alliance that helps in the process of reorganization and change following occurrence of a suicide attempt by a family member.[59] Alcoholism, depression, and marital conflict contribute to the production of pathologic intrafamilial relationships. The nature of adolescence with its requisite tasks of obtaining mastery, autonomy, and separation under parental guidance requires family involvement in both evaluation and treatment stages.

Families often can, when children cannot, provide information on peer relationships, sexual development, religious affiliations, sports, hobbies and other extracurricular activities. A mother, a father, a teacher and an adolescent provide different perspectives on relationships, symptoms, and functioning. The degree of mastery or lack of it pinpoints areas of strengths and weaknesses that can be used to develop individualized treatment plans. The goals of a plan should serve to reinforce strengths and change.

Finally, efforts should be made to identify any concurrent medical illness. Parents are more aware of developmental disabilities (dyslexia) which is a treatable risk factor for adolescent suicide. Frustration attendant with school failure despite superior cognitive capacity serves to precipitate or enhance dysphoria.

Treatment Plan

Management of a suicidal adolescent in a residential setting entails cooperation of a team of caregivers involved both within and without the setting. Once medical and psychiatric stability and safety are assured, definitive residential treatment commences. Structured therapy settings serve to mollify suicidal impulses by providing protection from family and peer tension, occasions of substance abuse, and sexual pressures, as well as afford opportunities for ventilation and receipt of help when self-destructive impulses emerge. Staff works with parents to allay fears of alienation and maintain opportunities for growth and reentry of the adolescent into the family system. Creating new coping skills concomitantly with reduction of family and peer stresses provides hope. Hope is critical to reduction of suicidal risk and successful social functioning without recurrence. Where major mental disorders exist such as bipolar disorder or schizophrenia, enhancing psychopharmacologic compliance is key to functioning. Families and all caregivers should be aware of diagnosis, course of illness, prognosis and expected results from therapeutic interventions.

Appropriate psychopharmacotherapy with tricyclic antidepressants, antianxiety agents, lithium, or neuroleptics where a mood disorder or psychosis is present is provided by the psychiatric consultant. Nursing staff and primary therapists provide support during the period of psychiatric stabilization. Once an adolescent is stabilized, the primary therapist begins to explore antecedents and conflicts leading up to the suicide attempt, fantasies about death, expected outcome (sympathy, guilt, or concern of family and friends), and personal denial of the finality of death.

Concurrent with individual therapy, the focus of family therapy should be on family dynamics that may have interfered with an adolescent's growth and separation from the family such as triangulation to relieve marital discord, parental collusion in facilitating self-destructive behavior such as undiagnosed parental alcoholism, and ineffective parenting. In the earlier instance there may have been an inability to set appropriate limits on unacceptable adolescent behavior or inability to set clear boundaries in interpersonal relationships. Degree of family pathology determines necessity of long term family therapy following discharge from the residential setting and the need for other strategic interventions (marital therapy for the conflicted couple, Alcoholics Anonymous and Al-Anon for the alcoholic family, supportive therapy and role modeling for the ineffective parent).

Specific treatment plans are required for patients with current alcohol or drug abuse and other psychiatric illness. Substance abuse may represent an attempt to self-medicate underlying depression or anxiety with suicidal ideation, or a patient may wish to die by suicide because of the uncontrollable craving for drugs or alcohol. In both cases substance abuse enhances, not diminishes, depression and self-destructive behavior.

Meetings of Cocaine Anonymous, Narcotics Anonymous, and Alcoholics Anonymous provide a theme through all phases of treatment: inpatient, partial hospital, residential, and outpatient. Where major psychiatric illness precedes substance abuse disorders, specific pharmacotherapy diminishes drive for drug and alcohol abuse but it is usually insufficient treatment in itself. Substance use becomes habitual regardless of the stimulus that generated the addictive behavior. Group therapy with a peer group provides means for confrontation with covert selfdestructive behavior through substance abuse. A group can be more effective at times than individual psychotherapy because the suicidal adolescent may be able to tolerate confrontation from his own peers better than from an adult therapist who may be perceived as colluding with or coopted by parents/adults and championing "the partyline." Individual therapy may be fraught with the anger and lack of cooperation because of projections onto the therapist as a parental substitute. Peer groups are composed of potential allies who share the mores, language and behavior of adolescence creating an alliance that can be used to therapeutic advantage.

Substance abusing adolescents require strict limit setting. Substance abusing adolescents *who are suicidal* require even more. Using drugs enhances depression and feeling out of control. Increased depression and lack of control results in augmentation of self-destructive drives, be it for chemical abuse or suicide attempts. Definitive contracts, where reasonably enforceable, are drawn up with families and patients.

Elements critical to an effective contract are:

1. random blood and urine screens for identification of illicit drug use using urine temperature to assure that a sample is fresh[60]
2. restriction to residence when required
3. room and person searches when deemed appropriate by staff, and
4. restriction of visitors to prevent acquisition of drugs

Contracts used in a residential setting may need to be modified to comport with varying realities of individual cases. Contracts allow staff to set appropriate therapeutic goals to control drug use as well as provide a behavioral model for parents to use when a patient is discharged.

Number and complexity of problems determines duration and type of discharge care required. With suicidal substance abusing and dually-diagnosed adolescents some form of continuing relationship with inpatient therapists or an outpatient therapist who has already established a therapeutic alliance serves to minimize noncompliance. Primary psychiatric disorders require psychiatric follow-up; family psychopathology, strategic family therapy; and individual psychopathology, individual psychotherapy. Family resources and motivation limit the type of follow-up care. Limited family resources may require supplementation by community resources. Reestablishing patient and family ties to church and other community organizations (Boy Scouts, Girl Scouts, 4-H Clubs, religious youth groups) are untapped accessible resources providing support, structure, and opportunities for growth, solidification of identity, and mastery for adolescents in transition to community living.

Social Support

A powerful force in diminishing or enhancing future self-destructive impulses is peer support or pressure. The overwhelming response adolescents provide when asked who they would turn to when considering suicide is a "friend."[51] If friends are dysthymic and flirt with death through drugs, anonymous sexual liaisons, or careless car and motorcycle driving, risk of harm is enhanced. If friends chosen are supportive and have a number of coping skills themselves, such as use of friends and family when in trouble, seeking professional help when necessary, and involvement in sports and church and temple activities, risk of future harm is lessened.

School Planning

Successful community placement is contingent on evaluation of learning disabilities, school planning, and educational remediation when required. Children and adolescents who are suicidal require more inpatient care and long term aftercare than their nonsuicidal patient peers. Undiagnosed learning disabilities enhance frustration, failure, and isolation. Identification of these at the time of a suicidal crisis and appropriate placement to maximize learning potential contributes to favorable prognosis.

Prognosis

Suicide attempts after discharge were often used to mobilize significant others to alter their living arrangements. Working gradually toward resolution of conflictual living arrangements serves to mollify suicidogenic stresses. The estimated 12,000 children age 15 and below admitted to psychiatric hospitals each year compared to depressed children and nonsuicidal controls with other psychopathology are believed to experience more life stress as they mature including disruptive family events resulting in losses and separations from important others.[50] Cohen-Sandler et al.[50] found in their study that whereas nonsuicidal children with psychopathology are often withdrawn, have suffered rejection by peers, and more often have lived apart from parents, suicidal children typically maintained contact with their families. Rage emerges from the intensity of these relationships. Nearly two-thirds had, in fact, made homicidal threats or gestures. Other studies confirm the fact that suicidal behavior typically occurs in an intensely stressful chaotic and unpredictable context. Children who feel helpless and incapable of making an impact by other means attempt to affect or coerce others through a suicidal attempt. Self-destructive behavior functions as an interpersonal coping strategy to punish, gain revenge, or control. Parents themselves appear to model and foster impulsive coping styles.

Compliance with treatment is a problem with adolescents. Noncompliant adolescents have poorer self images, are depressed, and have family problems. Two-thirds of one group of adolescents studied who attempted suicide did not follow through on recommended aftercare regardless of type of referral.[56] Those with previous attempts are least likely to follow through. Evidence suggests that implementation of a treatment plan is difficult for all adolescents but in particular for repeaters. If prevention of recurrence or of ultimate suicide is a goal, longer hospitalization or residential treatment must be considered.

PREVENTION

Primary prevention of adolescent suicide, i.e., prevention of the ideation and act entails enhancing social support and teaching copying styles to eliminate self-destructive behavior either as a method to effect change in a stressful situation or to terminate life rather than continue to endure the pain and persist in the struggle. Secondary prevention involves early recognition and treatment of individuals who are suicidal. This necessitates heightening parents, teachers, clergy, friends, and adolescents themselves to warning signs of lethal intent and encouraging concerned friends and family to seek help in a timely manner as a family. All innuendos are to be taken seriously. Giving away cherished items is the most obvious. Increasing withdrawal, failing grades, substance abuse, frequent accidents, and suicide equivalent behaviors, e.g., racing cars, are more subtle. Finally, after an attempt occurs, tertiary prevention efforts seek where a person has survived without undue physical impairment, to help a family realize that support and treatment is needed in this high risk group to prevent recurrence. While only a fraction of those who attempt suicide go on to die by their own hand, nearly all who die have attempted before. These are individuals at highest risk for future attempts. Evaluation and treatment in an atmosphere of reinforced social supports, without seeking to attribute blame is key to successful management.

Another less obvious need for prevention exists when a suicide stands to ignite a chain of suicides. This is the "Werther Effect" named after the impact of publication of *The Sorrows of Young Werther* by Goethe in 1874. The story of a young man who died by a self-inflicted gunshot wound in despondence over unrequited love set off a series of imitative suicides across the continent causing several principalities to ban it.[1] This phenomena is seen following the death of a person whose presence holds some symbolic meaning regardless of whether the death is by suicide or otherwise. This was reported both following the death by assassination of John Lennon and by appendicitis of Rudolph Valentino. Increase in suicide rate is thought to be directly related to the extent of publicity as quantified by length of news accounts and circulation of press carrying them and by extent of television coverage.[1]

Educating all members of a community as to the extent and causes of adolescent suicides, enhancing parent-child, teacher-child and friend-child communication, strengthening social supports, and working with adults to continue their parenting role together after dissolution of the companion/lover role in marriage are recognized means of primary prevention. Parental wars resonate within children who identify with both parents and make children feel bad and suffer low self-esteem. Children may not want to die but do want to end the pain. Suicide sadly ends both.

Talented, bright, attractive, and sensitive children suffer the loneliness of the long distant runner. Everyone needs social support. Unique children who are exceptionally talented, have a physical defect or learning disability, have famous or infamous parents, are aroused by same-sex rather than opposite sex friends, and are offspring of immigrants feel more isolated and bad. Enhancement of social bonding reduces isolation. Many children who are dysphoric do not know words to articulate the pain but nevertheless are driven by desire to ameliorate it. Facilitation of parent-child and peer communication through training in emotional literacy in schools leads to ventilation of pent-up emotion before it reaches self-destructive proportions and enables others to draw near to help.

REFERENCES

1. Eisenberg L: The epidemiology of suicide in adolescents. *Pediatr Ann*, 13:47-53, 1984.

2. Hingson R, Merrigan D, Heeren T: Effects of Massachusetts raising its legal drinking age from 18 to 20 on deaths from teenage homicide, suicide and nontraffic accidents. *Pediatr Clin North Am*, 32:221-232, 1985.

3. Pfeffer CR: *The Suicidal Child*. New York, Guilford Press, 1986.

4. Slaby AE: Prevention, early identification and management of adolescent suicidal behavior. *RI Med J*, 69:463-479, 1986.

5. Shaffer, D: Suicide in childhood and early adolescence. *J Child Psychol Psychiatry*, 15:275-291, 1974.

6. Shaffer D, Fisher P: The epidemiology of suicide in children and young adolescents. *J Am Acad Child Psychiat*, 20:545-565, 1981.

7. Kosky R: Childhood suicidal behavior. *J Child Psychol Psychiatry*, 24:457-468, 1983.

8. Jaffe R, Offord D: Suicidal behavior in childhood. *Can J Psychiatry*, 28:57-63, 1983.

9. Holden C: Youth suicide: new research focuses on a growing social problem. *Science*, 233:839-841, 1986.

10. Holinger PC: Adolescent suicide: an epidemiological study of recent trends. *Am J Psychiatry*, 135:754-756, 1978.

11. Husain SA, Vandiver T: *Suicide in Children and Adolescents*. New York, Spectrum Publications, 1984.

12. Garfinkel, BD, Froese A, Hood J: Parasuicide in children and adolescents. Paper presented at the Ontario Psychiatric Association Meeting, January 1979.

13. Garfinkel B, Froese A, Hood J: Suicide attempts in children and adolescents. *Am J Psychiat*, 139:1257-1261, 1982.

14. Pfeffer, CR: Self-destructive behavior in children and adolescents. *Psychiatr Clinics of N Amer*, 8:215-226, 1985.

15. Garfinkel B, Golombek H: Suicidal Behavior in Adolescence. In: *The Adolescent and Mood Disturbance*. New York, International University Press, 1983.

16. Slaby AE, Lieb J, Tancredi LR: *The Handbook of Psychiatric Emergencies (Third Edition)*. New York, Medical Examination Publishing Co., 1985.

17. Kashani JH, Keller MB, Solomon N et al: Double depression in adolescent substance users. *J Affect Dis*, 8:153-157, 1985.

18. Slaby AE, McGuire PL: Prevention of Child and Adolescent Suicide. *Fair Oaks Psychiatry Letter*, 4:65-74, 1986.

19. Slaby AE: Evaluation and Management of Suicide Potential and Attempts, in (Leigh H, Ed.) *Psychiatry in the Practice of Medicine*. Menlo Park, California, Addison-Wesley, 1981.

20. Slaby AE, Kramer P: Evaluating suicide potential. *Butler Review*, 5:2-8, 1985.

21. Mo Ho, J: Clinical considerations of biological correlates of suicide. *Suicide and Life-Threatening Behavior*, 16:83-102, 1986.

22. Pfeffer C, Conte H, Plutchek R, et al: Suicidal behavior in latency-age children. *J Am Acad Child Psychiatry*, 18:679-693, 1979.

23. Pfeffer C, Zuckerman S, Plutchik R, et al: Suicide behavior in normal school children: a comparison with child psychiatric inpatients. *J Am Acad Child Psychiatry*, 23:416-423, 1984.

24. Pfeffer CR: Self-destructive behavior in children and adolescents. *Psychiatri Clin North Am*, 8:125-226, 1985.

25. Tishler C, McKenry P: Intrapsychic symptom dimensions of adolescent suicide attempters. *J Fam Prac*, 16:731-734, 1983.

26. Shafii M, Shafii SL: Self-destructive, suicidal behavior, and completed suicide, in *Pathways of Human Development: Normal Growth and Emotional Disorders in Infancy, Childhood and Adolescence*. Edited by Shafii M, Shafii SL. New York, Thieme-Stratten, 1982.

27. Shafii M, Whittinghill Jr, Dolen DC, Pearson VD, Derrick A, Carrigan S: Psychological reconstruction of completed suicide in childhood and adolescence in *Suicide in the Young*. Edited by Sudak HS, Ford AB, Rushforth NB. Boston, John Wright-PSG, 1984.

28. Shafii M, Carrigan S, Whittinghill HR, Derrick A: Psychological autopsy of completed suicide in children and adolescents. *Am J Psychiatry*, 142:1061-1064, 1985.

29. Shafii M, Stelta-Lenarsky J, Derrick AM, Beckner C, Whittinghill JR: Comorbidity of mental disorders in the postmortem diagnosis of completed suicide in children and adolescents. *J Affective Disorders* (In Press).

30. DeMai D, Carandente F, Claudio R: Evaluation of circadian, ciroseptan and circannual periodicity of attempted suicides. *Chronobiologia*, 9:185-193, 1982.

31. Vandiver T, Husain SA: *Suicide in Children and Adolescents*. New York, SP Medical & Scientific Books, 1984.

32. Roy A: Suicide: a multidetermined act. *Psychiatr Clinics of N Amer*, 8:243-250, 1985.

33. Carlson GA, Cantwell DP: A survey of depressive symptoms, syndromes and disorders in a child psychiatric population. *J Child Psychol & Psychiat*, 21:19-25, 1980.

34. Sudak HS: *Suicide in the Young*. Littleton, MA, P.S.G. Publishing Co., 1985.

35. Garfinkel, BD, Slaby AE: *Children Who Kill Themselves*.

36. Adam KS: Attempted suicide. *Psychiat Clinics of N Amer*, 8:183-201, 1985.

37. Coldney R: Are young women who attempt suicide hysterical? *Brit J Psychiat*, 138:141-146, 1981.

38. Hawton K, O'Grady J, Osborn M, Cole D: Adolescents who take overdoses: their characteristics, problems, and contacts with helping agencies. *Brit J Psychiat*, 140:118-123, 1982.

39. Hawton K, Cole D, O'Grady J, Osborn M: Motivational aspects of deliberate self-poisoning in adolescents. *Brit Psychiat*, 141:286-291, 1982.

40. Rydelius PA: Deaths among child and adolescent psychiatric patients. *Acta Psychiat Scand*, 70:119-126, 1984.

41. Taylor E, Stansfield S: Children who poison themselves: a clinical comparison with psychiatric controls. *Brit J Psychiat*, 145:127-135, 1984.

42. Kellner CH, Best CC, Roberts JM, Bjorksten O: Self-destructive behavior in hospitalized medical and surgical patients. *Psychiat Clinics of N Amer*, 8:279-280, 1985.

43. Galanter M, Castaneda R: Self-destructive behavior in the substance abuser. *Psychiat Clinics of N Amer*, 8:251-261, 1985.

44. Adam K, Lohrenz J, Harper D, Streiner D: Early parental loss and suicidal ideation in university students. *Can J Psychiat*, 27:275-281, 1982.

45. Hacker SJ: Self-harmful sexual behavior. *Psychiat Clinics of N Amer*, 8:323-337, 1985.

46. Motto J: Development of a suicide risk assessment instrument. Paper read at 15th Annual Meeting of the American Association of Suicidology, New York, NY, April 16, 1982.

47. Pattison EM, Kaha J: The deliberate self-harm syndrome. *Am J Psychiat*, 140:867-872, 1983.

48. Salk L, Sturner W, Lipsitt L, Reilly B, Levat R: Relationship of maternal and perinatal conditions to eventual adolescent suicide. *The Lancet*, 624-626, March 16, 1985.

49. Clayton PJ: Suicide. *Psychiatr Cliln North Am*, 8:703-214, 1985.

50. Cohen-Sandler R, Berman A, King R: A follow-up study of hospitalized suicidal children. *J Am Acad Child Psychiatry*, 21:398-403, 1982.

51. Emery P: Adolescent depression and suicide. *Adolescence*, 18:245-258, 1983.

52. Robins E: The final months: a study of the lives of 134 persons who committed suicide. New York, Oxford University Press, 1981.

53. Tuckman J, Connor H: Attempted suicide in adolescents. *Am J Psychiatry*, 119:228-232, 1982.

54. Roy A: Suicide and psychiatric patients. *Psychiat Clinics of N Amer*, 8:227-241, 1985.

55. Roy A: Suicide: a multidetermined act. *Psychiat Clinics of N Amer*, 8:243-250, 1985.

56. Litt I, Cushey W, Rudd S: Emergency room evaluation of the adolescent who attempts suicide: compliance with follow-up. *J Adolesc Health Care*, 4:106-108, 1983.

57. Pepitone-Arrcola-Rockwell D, Core N: Fifty-two medical student suicides. *Am J Psychiatry*, 138:198-201, 1981.

58. Salk L, Sturner W, Lipsitt L, Reilly B, Levat R: Relationship of maternal and perinatal conditions to eventual adolescent suicide. *Lancet*, 624-626, March 16, 1985.

59. Raymond ME, Slaby AE, Lieb J: The Healing Alliance. New York, Norton, 1975.

60. Ehrenkrantz, J: Fake urine samples for drug analysis: hot, but not hot enough. *JAMA* 259:841, 1988.

61. Deykin EY, Hsieh CC, Joshi N, et al: Adolescent suicidal and self-destructive behavior: results of an intervention study. *J Adolesc Health Care*, 7:88-95, 1986.

BIOGRAPHICAL NOTES

Andrew Slaby graduated from Columbia University College of Physicians and Surgeons and Yale University, and holds MD, MPH, and PhD degrees. He is Medical Director of Fair Oaks Hospital, Adjunct Professor of Psychiatry and Human Behavior at Brown University, and Clinical Professor of Psychiatry at New York University and the New York Medical College. He has written many scientific books, papers and research studies, and received many scientific prizes and awards. He is particularly interested in personal crisis intervention and management, suicide prevention, management of violent individuals, and the techniques of adaptation to life.

Patricia McGuire was trained in psychiatry at Johns Hopkins University and Harvard before joining the staff at Fair Oaks Hospital. She is especially interested in the psychiatric manifestations of medical illness and seasonal mood disorders.

Adolescent Suicide in a Residential Treatment Center: A Clinical and Administrative Post-Mortem

Danilo E. Ponce, MD
Jeff P. Smith, MA

SUMMARY. The impact of a successful suicide by a resident in a Residential Treatment Center (RTC) could be potentially catastrophic, if not handled sensitively and competently. This paper describes the experiences of a RTC in which a successful suicide of an adolescent male resident did occur, delineating steps taken to prevent or minimize the catastrophic aftermath from happening. A retrospective analysis and rationale for the interventions that were implemented are presented for discussion. The paper concludes with a suggestion of things to remember and a list of "Do's and Don'ts."

By all measures, suicides exact a heavy emotional toll inflicting long-lasting, perhaps permanent psychological wounds on the survivors (Rogers, 1982; Calhoun, 1984; Hatton, 1981). If the person who committed the felo-de-se happens to be a youngster in a treatment institution, the impact on the survivors increases exponentially for the following reasons:

Danilo E. Ponce is Professor and Director of Child Psychiatry Training, University of Hawaii, John A. Burns Medical School, Department of Psychiatry. Jeff Smith is Program Services Director of The Salvation Army Residential Treatment Facilities For Children and Youth in Honolulu, HI.

This paper was originally presented at the 31st Annual Meeting of the American Association of Children's Residential Centers, New Orleans, LA, October 15-17, 1987.

45

1. one has to take into account the effect(s) the suicide had on the other equally, if not more disturbed, residents
2. one has to consider the reactions of staff who are professionally accountable for the care and treatment of the residents in the center
3. one has to contend not only with the members of the bereaved family, but with the families of the other residents
4. one has to consider the medico-legal liability issues, which, if not raised by the surviving family, may be raised (and rightfully so) by funding and accrediting agencies
5. there is the subtle, but nonetheless ubiquitous impact of the suicide on the professional and lay community vis-à-vis the professional and public image of the RTC

Our RTC was dramatically introduced to the above realities of suicide when a 15 year old male resident hung himself in the laundry room of the unit in which he was staying. We said "dramatically," because our RTC was 8 years old at that time and we did not have any experience at all dealing with a suicide (and have not had one since) prior to that incident. There was the usual number of suicide gestures by residents, but they were all relatively trivial, and were handled in a routine fashion. The suddenness, the relative ease, and the success of the young man's suicide caught us off guard. The inevitable need to deal with the tragic effects on the "survivors," with no previous experience to guide us, and relying mostly on our clinical abilities, provided the stimulus for us to shed our professional naiveté, and instilled the necessary impetus that eventually enabled us to re-think our stance as a treating agency regarding the possibility of suicide in our RTC.

We will not describe a protracted analysis of the youngster's suicide — the literature is already extensive (see for example Holinger, 1978; Rosenkrantz, 1978; DenHouter, 1981; Jenkins, 1982; Reis, 1984; Copeland, 1985; Gispert, 1985; Gorkin, 1985; Hodgman, 1985; Shulman, 1985; Greene, 1986; Pfeffer, 1986) — instead, we would like to share what we learned from the incident in the form of principles that address the five variables mentioned earlier. To our knowledge, there is not a single article currently available that deals with the latter issues in a systematic fashion.

DEALING WITH OTHER RESIDENTS

"Copy-cat" suicides in the "normal" adolescent population accounts for the rash of suicides immediately following a well-publicized teenage suicide, as recent events have demonstrated (Time, 1987). Needless to say, in RTC's we are interacting with a population that is more disturbed, highly mercurial, and eminently more impressionable. The risks for contagion are therefore enhanced tremendously, if not properly contained. Hence, the first item of concern to staff in the event of a suicide, is to minimize and contain group contagion. The second major consideration is how to handle the impact of the suicide on each of the individual residents vis-à-vis their own unique psychopathology. Undoubtedly, each one of them will respond differently, depending on their unique clinical situation, i.e., their diagnosis, psychopathology, developmental stage, and their relationship with the deceased. The third, and perhaps the most important consideration in the long run, is the fact that regardless of the uniqueness of their clinical status, they are confronted once again with the loss process. Most, if not all of them, have been damaged by "goodbyes" that are rather traumatic, abrupt or protracted, and guilt inducing—leaving them with an unresolved and festering mourning process. The following are some of the steps we took, and in retrospect, some steps we might have taken, to address these three issues:

1. Minimize group contagion—This should be done immediately to minimize spread of rumors, and other false or misleading information. What we did was to gather all the youngsters in each of the units (we have three: pre-adolescent boys; adolescent girls; and adolescent boys), and had the Unit Supervisors describe as factually as possible the circumstances surrounding the suicide (Who, What, When, Where, How). We debated whether to do this with all of them assembled in one big group, or to do it by units. In the end, we decided to do it by units. This enabled us to tailor presentation of the "facts" to suit the population of the unit. For example, with the pre-adolescent boys, a simple and concrete description of the facts appeared to be sufficient. With the more abstract and sophisti-

cated adolescent boys and girls, more information was needed, such as whether the police were called, whether attempts to resuscitate him were made, etc. In either case, the supervisors and the staff were instructed to de-emphasize gory details, and certainly, to refrain from going into discussions of motivation, or attempts at analysis, explanations or inferences. Speculations, in our opinion, merely perpetuate an aura of uncertainty and anxiety.

2. Individual youngsters — Following the group meeting, counselors and their counselees were broken-up into individual or small groups to deal with the impact of the suicide on a more personal basis. This provided the transition, and in retrospect, the cushion, that enabled the youngsters to deal ultimately with loss issues.

3. Dealing with loss — A rule of thumb in coping with loss is the so-called 3 "E's": Loss must be Experienced, Expressed, Endured. Experiencing loss means allowing the youngsters to feel the impact of the suicide in their own special way, in a manner that is clinically appropriate to each of them. There is a common albeit misguided belief even among professionals, in the therapeutic benefits of catharsis ("let it all hang out"). This is simply not so, even dangerous, with some of the youngsters we treat in RTCs. With borderline youngsters, for example, the most prudent thing to do might be to reinforce their defenses, e.g., denial, or to give an extra dose of tranquilizers to alleviate their already tenuous hold on reality. Similarly, careful thought must be given to the appropriate context (individual, group, family) by which loss is to be expressed and the form it takes (talking, crying, hugging). As in any other clinical context, expression is not to be confused with a license to "act out." Firm limit-setting based on overall clinical considerations must prevail; the overall message given to the youngsters has to be that the pain of loss is to be endured without resorting to acting out, and, like a wound, staff can only provide support and serve as psycho-social anodynes, but in the final analysis, the youngsters will have to endure the pain themselves.

4. The topic of depression and mourning/loss as part of a planned

Health and Sex-Education curriculum—Though we have not, as yet, incorporated these topics in our classes, plans are underway to do so. This is more of a long-term, preventive measure.

Depending on how the youngsters respond to these immediate interventions, decisions can then be made on whether further steps are necessary beyond those that are part of day-to-day programming. This includes considerations regarding who will participate in the funeral services, and in what capacity. Attending the services may not necessarily be therapeutic for all the residents, and decisions should be based on individual clinical considerations.

STAFF ISSUES

Like the youngsters, staff will have their own unique reactions to the suicide depending on their respective personalities, their position in the organization, their clinical maturity, and the kind of relationship they had with the deceased. To a certain extent, they will also have to undergo the grief work described by Lindemann (1965). According to Lindemann, the work essentially consists of four stages: Denial, Anger, Guilt, and the final stage of Resolution which is a redefinition of the survivor's relationship with the deceased.

Suicide as a traumatic event is catastrophic enough by itself, but in addition, the staff is being asked, implicitly or explicitly, to take care of their own grief work in addition to creating a therapeutic emotional climate that will allow the disturbed youngsters to proceed with their recovery. This may be asking too much, especially from staff who may feel that they were "negligent," and hence, indirectly responsible for the youngster's death. A comprehensive approach must, therefore, include not only a plan for the youngsters, but also a formal plan designed to sensitively respond to staff needs (Gross, 1979).

From an organizational standpoint, there are two major issues that require immediate and sustained attention in the event of a catastrophe. These two issues in turn generate problems on the part of the staff which must be reckoned with by the administration. These two issues are technical and psycho-social in nature. The technical issues encumber the "business" side of what must be done (implementation of administrative, bureaucratic and logistical procedures). Having a clearly articulated, action-oriented plan that deals with the technical issues, is probably the most therapeutic step administration can do for the staff during the first few hours and days following the suicide. Providing a sense of direction and making them do meaningful work, enables staff to feel empowered and useful. This combats the possibility of paralyzing inaction which could ensue as a result of too much preoccupation with their own grief work.

Psycho-social issues consist of the more humane aspects of the situation. We did not pay too much attention to this facet of comprehensive planning then, but we have since given some thought on the matter, particularly as it applies to the staff, and we subsequently came up with four over-arching principles. These principles served us in good stead, as we recently had the occasion to put the principles in operation following the grisly murder of a recently discharged youngster from our Center:

1. Permission must be given to line-staff to express their own grief in ways that they feel comfortable with other staff, as well as with the youngsters.
2. Psycho-social assistance must be made available to staff who feel they may need it. In this regard, the offer must not be vague or general. As much as possible, the offer should be explicit, leaving enough room for staff to make independent decisions ("I have talked to Dr. X, and he/she has agreed to be available to you at Y time should you need assistance in sorting out your feelings.").
3. Brief description to staff of the expected grief work (using Lindemann's 1965 schema) that youngsters are expected to undergo; possible extreme reactions they might observe, and suggested ways of intervening with these reactions. Most importantly, staff must be made aware that the grief process is equally applicable to them, and they need to be informed of agency resources that could assist them with their own grief work.

4. A psychological post-mortem (Neill, 1974; Shafii, 1985) on the suicide done by the most respected and senior clinician of the agency, shared with, and read by all staff within a few weeks or so, is very helpful in putting closure on the process. The post-mortem should help the staff in their need to understand the tragic event, and perhaps alleviate any lingering sense of guilt in some staff.

DEALING WITH THE BEREAVED FAMILY AND FAMILIES OF OTHER RESIDENTS

In RTCs, one must cope with the impact of the suicide not only with the immediate family members of the deceased (Hatton, 1981; Pfeffer, 1982; Calhoun, 1984), but with the families of the other residents as well. Though the impact may be of a different kind, it is nonetheless reasonable to expect that the families of other residents will have some feelings about the suicide particularly as it revolves around their son/daughter/relative. Questions of safety and security, effectiveness of treatment services, competency of staff etc., arise quite naturally, especially if lurking behind these questions is an unspoken anxiety that "there but for the grace of God, goes my son/daughter."

Suggested ways of therapeutically intervening with the bereaved family have been amply documented in the literature (Hatton, 1981; Pfeffer, 1982; Rogers, 1982). The Center ought to be sensitive to their needs and their highly emotional and vulnerable state, otherwise the incident might have potentially disastrous consequences later on, including costly legal ramifications. In our particular case, the Program Services Director informed the parents with the facts of the situation. Note who makes the initial call — somebody important enough to communicate that the Center cares — but not the top executive, who should be available later on if the family has further questions. Following a brief and cursory explanation of bureaucratic procedures that needed to be done, the rest of his communication was spent not only on expressions of sorrow and regret, but on action-oriented offers of assistance.

Counselors, therapists, and administrators were made available to the family, at their convenience, to use in any manner they chose. The family therapists of the youngster were especially help-ful in putting things in perspective, while serving as an emotional refuge for the bereaved family. All that can be done to assist the family to deal with technical and bureaucratic red-tape was done, including assisting them in making arrangements for funeral ser-vices. Finally, we offered to continue seeing the family for as long as they needed our services. These services were offered even though technically we were not obligated to do so, and wouldn't be recompensed for the services. They appreciated the offer, but gra-ciously declined it.

As far as the families of the other residents were concerned, we gave them information on a "need-to-know" basis, making sure that patient confidentiality was preserved. All communications were gently steered towards discussions that were relevant to their particular child, and any reference to the youngster who committed suicide was deemphasized. Families who expressed a desire to par-ticipate in the funeral services were supported and encourage to do so, following permission from the bereaved family. Families who may have had lingering feelings about the suicide were asked to bring these to their respective counselors or therapists.

DEALING WITH LIABILITY ISSUES

In the olden days, the prevalent view was that suicide was an abominable sin against God, and a heinous crime against the king. Hence, suicide was originally a felony in English common law pun-ishable by a shameful burial at the cross-roads of a public highway, with a stake through the heart, and a stone on the face of the corpse (Williams, 1968). In addition, the deceased's estate was forfeited to the king (Drukteinis, 1985). The times have changed, indeed, since those days. Suicide is now seen primarily as an involuntary act, and the prevailing medico-legal trend is to find someone/somebody to blame, either for causing it, or for failing to prevent it. Like it or not, RTCs will need to pay particular attention (if they have not done so already) to the "negligence" aspect of suicides assuming, of course, that they won't be held liable for "causing" it. In just 5 years (1978-1983), claims against psychiatrists have doubled (from 2% to 4%), and in 18% of these claims, negligence leading to suicide was invoked. One percent of suicides occur in hospitals, with 1/3 of the cases resulting in lawsuits; 1/2 of which were against the hospitals (Litman, 1982).

Liability for failing to prevent suicide is based on "the breach of a specific affirmative duty of care owed to the person committing the suicide" (Schwartz, 1971). For a professional—a psychiatrist, for example—this means a failure to conform to appropriate medical practice, or to utilize appropriate clinical judgement. For an institution—a RTC, for example—this means staff not conforming to orders, not following institutional policy, or not reporting significant information to the treating professional(s) (Perr, 1985). Rachlin (1984) has an ingenious mnemonic for remembering the general principles involved in litigation for negligence in suicides. He calls it the "4 D's": Dereliction of-Duty-Directly causing-Damages (suicide).

Theoretically, anybody who has been made privy to information regarding a potential suicide is liable, because of the vagueness as to what constitutes "duty of care": liquor dispensers, jailers, pharmacists, counselors, employers, hotel managers, attorneys, and yes, even the parents themselves (Schwartz, 1971). The bone of contention here is "breach of a special duty of care," and in this regard, two legal words should be remembered: "foreseeable," and "predictable." Foreseeability is a subjective likelihood that an event is to occur. Predictability is a statistical probability that an event is to occur (Drukteinis, 1985). Liability is based on the premise that unless the suicide was reasonably foreseeable, it is highly unlikely that the professional or the institution was negligent. That is to say, if the suicide could not reasonably be foreseen, no steps to prevent it are indicated, and liability is not likely to be found. Conversely, if the professional and/or the institution have reason to believe that the suicide was a possibility, then they should have taken steps to prevent it. Putting it somewhat differently, if the suicide was, or can be foreseen or predicted, and a proximate cause can be established between the suicide and acts of omission or commission, then the professional or institution is liable (Rachlin, 1984). "Proximate cause" is a "but for" or a "without which" proposition. "This suicide would not have occurred but for the questioned act(s) or omission(s), or the questioned act(s) or omission(s) is/are the intervention(s) without which the suicide would not have occurred."

The reasonable and prudent principles to bear in mind in addressing the issue of suicide in a RTC are:

1. Suicide policies and procedures—The first item that will be scrutinized in the event of an attempt or a successful suicide is the presence or absence of coherent policies (the "What"), and procedures (the "How To") to implement the policies. At a bare minimum, policies should address how potential suicides are to be "foreseen" or "predicted" (Rotheram, 1987), and when detected, how they are to be prevented. Policies should also state the position of the institution regarding successful attempts, and procedures to deal with the aftermath. Criteria will need to be explicitly stated for determining suicidality, with clear delineation of staff responsibility, i.e., "Who does What to Whom, Where, When, How," once suicide potential is established. In the unfortunate event of a successful suicide, explicit procedures should be available to serve as a guide for action plans designed to manage the rest of the patient population; the staff (both administrative and clinical staff); the aggrieved family, and families of other patients; participating agencies; and the community-at-large.

2. Record Keeping—Suits are won or lost on the basis of adequate documentation. Orders and carrying out of orders must be studiously documented in the official records. Progress Notes must distinguish between what is observation ("He has lost 10 pounds during the past two weeks"), and what is clinical inference or opinion (". . . and this could indicate an underlying depression."). In this regard, staff must be carefully educated about not using the word "suicidal" too loosely or too lightly because once somebody notes it anywhere on the official chart, it becomes public domain. Changes in privilege status ought to be recorded in the chart, with the accompanying reasons for doing so. The conflict between giving a suicidal patient some degree of "freedom" with its attendant liabilities versus putting him in restraints could be easily resolved with proper documentation, i.e., writing explicitly the thera-

peutic reasons for either one; the issue then becomes a matter of clinical judgement, rather than negligence, should a patient who was given some freedom commit suicide in the process.

3. Communication system—Although lines of communication should be explicit in any organization, it deserves special attention in policies or procedures regarding suicide. Mechanisms for collecting and disseminating information should be specific, unambiguous and known to all staff. For example, if the institutional cook just happened to overhear a youngster say "I'm going to kill myself tonight" to whom should he/she pass this information along? In what form (Memo? Telephone call?) and does he/she ever get any feedback later on, as to what was done with his/her information?

4. Physical plant monitoring—Here again, although maintaining an optimal therapeutic milieu should be part of the standards covering the total institution, the presence of suicidal patients highlights the need for scrupulous adherence to these standards. For example, are there exposed pipes that could be utilized to hang oneself? What about razor blades? When was the last time a survey was made of the milieu?

INTERACTING WITH THE PROFESSIONAL AND LAY COMMUNITY

There is probably not much the Center can do, nor is there much to be done in this area except to mention it as a potential source of problems. The media, to their credit, have generally shied away from publicizing these occurrences. Referring agencies and professionals, however, will naturally express some concerns regarding their referrals, much like the families of the other residents. Hence, there should be a procedure to insure that inquiries are handled expeditiously in a professional, non-defensive, reassuring, and courteous manner. There should be a staff member (in our case, the Program Services Director) that is assigned to field all calls and inquiries, and a roster of alternate staff in case the designated staff becomes unavailable. The designated staff ought to have a substantial knowledge of the case, up-to-date information regarding circumstances surrounding the suicide, a grasp of overall treatment programming, and authority to make on-the-spot decisions. Needless to say, he/she should have the requisite communication skills to be able to read and respond appropriately to nuances of communication. The period immediately following the suicide is an emotionally-laden, highly volatile period, and any delays in responding to inquiries, seeming defensiveness, indecision, or lack of solid information will reflect very badly on the institution. Telephone operators and secretaries should know the whereabouts of the designated staff at most times, and if he/she is unable to respond to calls, a definite time should be established when he/she can return the call. We have learned our lesson well regarding the importance of having a communication center during highly charged situations in the past, when we had to painfully untangle the negative consequences of a call that was not returned, or not returned on time; a call taken by staff not authorized or equipped to do so; or by confusion on the part of telephone operators as to whom to give the call.

CONCLUSIONS

There are no currently available statistics that will give us a reliable picture of the incidence or prevalence of suicides in RTCs. There is a significant increase of adolescent suicides in the general population such that suicide is now the second leading cause of death during the teenage years (12.8 per 100,000 by 1984, compared to 5.1 per 100,000 in 1960 — National Center for Health Statistics, 1984). Our experience seems to parallel the national trend. During the past ten years, we have witnessed an upsurge of youngsters admitted wherein suicide risk played a major role in their psychopathology. We have already observed a 16% increase of youngsters admitted with suicidal thinking as a major referral concern during the last six years: 23 out of 87 youngsters from 1982-84 (26%); 32 out of 76 from 1985 to July 1987 (42%). Five year comparisons also show a steady increase: 43 of 163 youngsters from 1978-82 (26%); 48 of 137 from 1983 to July 1987 (35%) — already a 9% increase. If the national statistics and our experience is any indication of a prevailing trend, then RTCs will have to pay closer attention to the possibility of suicide occurring during a youngster's tenure in an RTC. Culling from our own experience in coping with the suicide of one of our residents, we have isolated five areas of concern together with some guidelines as to how a RTC might address these areas. Summarizing these guidelines in the form of "Do's" and "Don'ts" are:

DO

- Have a checklist of "things to do" that covers the other residents; the staff; the bereaved family and the families of other residents; preventing liability; and finally, dealing with the professional and lay community. This checklist should contain "technical" things to do, and "human/humane" things to do.
- Insure that policies and procedures regarding suicide are kept up-to-date through at least annual reviews to insure they are reasonable and reflective of the need for accurate, comprehensive and timely documentation.
- Insure that mechanisms are geared to mobilize an effective communication system in the event of a suicide.
- Understand that this is a highly volatile situation for everyone, and that an ounce of prevention is worth a pound of cure.

DON'T

- Have a defensive posture and organize your planning solely around preventing liability. Ironically, it is in being too legalistic at times, that brings on the very thing that the institution wants to avoid at all costs.
- Get too preoccupied with fixing guilt and blame, nor indulge too much in armchair speculation of motivations, dynamics, etc. Action is especially important during the first few hours and days following the tragic event.
- Think that it is healthy for everybody to have a catharsis, or for that matter, that there is a "right" way of expressing grief and loss.
- Think that because suicide is a catastrophic event, that it is a fait accompli for catastrophic reactions to occur. Youngsters

and junior staff generally reflect the overall emotional climate of their environs — if the climate is calm, professional, competent, and supportive, the process is usually endured and resolved with little or no untoward reactions.

REFERENCES

Calhoun LG et al. Suicidal Death: Social Reactions to Bereaved Survivors. *The Journal of Psychology*, 116:255-261, 1984.

Copeland AR. Childhood Suicide: A Report of Four Cases. *Journal of Forensic Scenes*, 30(3):965-967, 1985.

Den Houter KV. To Silence One's Self: A Brief Analysis of the Literature on Adolescent Suicide. *Child Welfare*, 60(1):2-10, 1981.

Drukteinis AM. Psychiatric Perspectives on Civil Liability for Suicide. *Bull Am Acad Psychiatry Law*, 13(1):71-83, 1985.

Gispert M et al. Suicide Adolescents: Factors in Evaluation. *Adolescence*, 20(8):753-762, 1985.

Gorkin M. On The Suicide of One's Patient. *Bulletin of the Meninger Clinic*, 49(1):1-9, 1985.

Greene JW et al. Depression and Suicide in Children and Adolescents. *Comprehensive Therapy*, 12(2):38-43, 1986.

Gross G. The Child Care Workers Response To The Death of a Child. *Child Care Quarterly*, 8(1):59-66, 1979.

Hatton CL et al. Bereavement Group for Parents Who Suffered a Suicidal Loss of a Child. *Suicide and Life Threatening Behavior*, 11(3):141-150, 1981.

Hodgman CH. Recent Findings in Adolescent Depression and Suicide. *Developmental and Behavioral Pediatrics*, 6(3):162-170, 1985.

Holinger PC. Adolescent Suicide: An Epidemiological Study of Recent Trends. *Am J Psychiatry*, 135(6):754-756, 1978.

Jenkins RL et al. The Risk and Prevention of Suicide in Residential Treatment of Adolescents. *Juvenile and Family Court Journal*, 33(2):11-16, 1982.

Lindemann E. Symptomatology and Management of Acute Grief. *Crisis Intervention*, New York, 1965.

Litman R. Hospital Suicides: Lawsuits and Standards. *Suicide and Life Threatening Behavior*, 12:212-220, 1982.

National Center for Health Statistics. *Vital Statistics of the US*, Washington D.C., 1984.

Neill K et al. The Psychological Autopsy: A Technique for Investigating a Hospital Suicide. *Hospital and Community Psychiatry*, 25(1):33-36, 1974.

Perr IN. Suicide Litigation and Risk Management: A Review of 32 Cases. *Bull Am Acad Psychiatry Law*, 13(3):209-219, 1985.

Pfeffer CR. Intervention for Suicidal Children and Their Parents. *Suicide and Life Threatening Behavior*, 12(4):240-248, 1982.

Pfeffer CR. Modalities of Treatment for Suicidal Children: An Overview of the Literature on Current Practice. *Am J of Psychotherapy*, 37(3):364-372.

Pfeffer CR et al. Suicidal Behavior in Child Psychiatric Inpatients and Outpatients and in Nonpatients. *Am J of Psychiatry*, 143(6):733-738, 1986.

Rachlin S. Double Jeopardy: Suicide and malpractice. *General Hospital Psychiatry*, 6(4):302-307, 1984.

Reis, K. & Resnick, D. Adolescent Suicidal Behavior: A Residential Treatment Center View. *Res Group Care Treatment*, 2(4):21-34, 1984.

Rogers J et al. Help for Families of Suicide: Survivors Support Program. *Can J Psychiatry*, 27(6):444-449, 1982.

Rosenkrantz AL. A Note on Adolescent Suicide: Incidence, Dynamics and Some Suggestions for Treatment. *Adolescence*, 13(5):209-214, 1978.

Rotheram MJ. Evaluation of Imminent Danger for Suicide Among Youth. *Am J Orthopsychiat*, 57(1):102-110, 1987.

Schwartz VE. Civil Liability for Causing Suicide: A Synthesis of Law and Psychiatry. *Vanderbilt Law Review*, 24:217, 1971.

Shafii M et al. Psychological Autopsy of Completed Suicides in Children and Adolescents. *Am J Psychiatry*, 142(9):1061-1064, 1985.

Shulman S et al. Suicidal Behavior at School: A Systemic Perspective. *Journal of Adolescence*, 8(3):263-269, 1985.

Time Magazine. Teen Suicide, March 23:12-13, 1987.

Williams GL. The Sanctity of Life and the Criminal Law. New York: Knopf, 259, 1968.

BIOGRAPHICAL NOTE

Dr. Danilo Ponce is a child psychiatrist, a professor at the University of Hawaii, and Medical/Clinical Services Director of the Salvation Army Residential Treatment Facilities for Children and Youth. He is particularly interested in the transcultural aspects of mental health and the integration of Eastern (for example, Buddhism) and Western psychologies as they relate to clinical practice. He has written papers on the clinical use of meditation with children.

Completed Suicide in Children and Adolescents: A Review

Harry M. Hoberman, PhD

COMPLETED SUICIDE IN YOUTH

Suicide among adolescents has emerged as a significant public health problem. As Blum (1987) notes, adolescents are the only age group in the United States who have not experienced improvement in their health status over the last 30 years. In particular, he has pointed out that violence has emerged as the primary cause of death among young persons, with accidents, homicides, and suicides accounting for over 77% of adolescent deaths. Of the three possible causes of death, suicide is perhaps most disturbing because it involves some volitional element. It raises the question, why would young people who are just beginning to experience life choose to end it? Consequently, suicide among the young is an emotionally charged phenomenon; it elicits sadness over the loss, guilt over whether it could have been prevented, anger at the apparent rejection, and finally, anxiety about the possibility of another such death.

Until recently, accurate knowledge of the characteristics of youthful suicide completers has been quite limited. As recently as 1982, a review of the literature identified only two data-based studies of the characteristics of child or adolescent suicide (Berman & Cohen-Sandler, 1982). Instead, the field has been dominated by speculation and the influence of relatively few cases which reach

---

Harry M. Hoberman is Assistant Professor of Psychiatry, Adolescent Health Program, Pediatrics and Child Development, University of Minnesota.

61

public attention. Both the public as well as professionals possess erroneous conceptions of the nature of suicidal behavior among the young. Potential misconceptions have significant implications since they may determine the content and structure of intervention programs directed at potentially suicidal youth. Consequently, there is a pressing need for systematic information delineating the characteristics of children and adolescents who commit suicide. The purpose of the chapter is to systematically review and integrate the findings of the increasing number of studies which attempt to describe groups of young suicides.

Beyond Jan-Tausch's (1964) initial study of 41 child and adolescent suicides, nine studies have carefully attempted to delineate factors associated with self inflicted death among younger persons in Western societies. Schaffer (1974) studied children 14 and under who had committed suicide in England and Wales between 1962 and 1968 (n = 31). Cosand, Bourque, and Krauss (1982) presented descriptive data on 315 suicides between the ages of 10 and 24 in Sacramento County, California from 1950 to 1979. Pettifor and colleagues (1983) described differences between 40 adolescents seen at a mental health clinic in Alberta, between 1946 and 1980, who eventually committed suicide (between 1956 and 1979) and a matched group of nonsuicidal clinic outpatients. Garfinkel and Golombek (1983) examined coroners' and police reports and collected information on 1,554 suicides by persons aged 10 to 24 in Ontario. Poteet (1987) studied medical examiners' reports for 87 suicides (ages 13-19) which occurred between 1970 and 1985 in Tennessee. Shaffi, Carrigan, Whittinghill and Derrick (1985) described the results of "psychological autopsies" conducted on 20 persons aged 19 and under. Finally, Thompson (1987) reported on 190 suicides by persons aged less than 20 in Manitoba from 1970 to 1982. Brent, Perper, Goldstein, Kolko, Allan, Allman, and Zelenak (1988) compared 27 adolescent suicide victims to 56 suicidal psychiatric inpatients. Hoberman and Garfinkel (1988) reviewed the medical examiner's records for 229 suicides under the age of 20. Schaffer (1985; in Holden, 1986) has described preliminary results of his ongoing study of 160 adolescent suicide completers in the metropolitan New York area.

Each of these studies has contributed to the understanding of youth suicide. Yet it must be noted that these investigations possess certain methodological limitations. Several involve relatively small numbers of subjects, while some are based upon archival review and not up on psychological autopsies. A number of studies include persons whose suicides occurred a number of years ago, raising the question of potential cohort differences. Given the increasing rates of youth suicide over the last 30 years (C.D.C., 1986), the characteristics of the youth who has recently taken his or her life may be quite different from one who committed suicide a number of decades ago. A number of studies fail to characterize sex differences or age differences within the larger group of adolescent suicides; even when such differences are reported, statistical comparisons may not have been conducted which leaves doubt as to the valid nature of such distinctions. If such differences exist then their value as diagnostic criteria may be obscured by discussions of adolescent suicide in general. Both Hawton (1986) and Schaffer and Fisher (1981) have argued that suicides are often under-reported; Hoberman and Garfinkel (1988), in surveying all youthful deaths from non-natural causes over a ten year period found that medical examiners' misidentified actual suicides 15% of the time. Thus, samples of suicide victims may not always be representative of the larger population of suicide completers. Several methodological issues therefore, may compromise the application of the limited knowledge available concerning child and adolescent suicides. By comparing and contrasting all of the available studies in this area, it is hoped that a more comprehensive and uniform picture of youth suicide will emerge.

EPIDEMIOLOGY

In 1980, 3,442 persons aged 15 to 19 committed suicide. For adolescents, in 1950, the rate of suicide per 100,000 population was 2.7; by 1980, it had reached 8.5 (C.D.C., 1986). This constitutes an increase of 215%. Suicide rates in this group appear to have increased again in the mid-1980s; by 1985, the rate per 100,000 was 10.0 (C.D.C., 1987). Youth suicide rates appear to demonstrate a cohort effect, with more recently born young persons demonstrating increasingly higher rates (Murphy & Wetzel, 1980; Cosand et al., 1982). Older adolescents are clearly at greater risk for suicide compared to younger persons with that risk increasing in a linear fashion. Schaffer (1974) found no suicides under the age of 12, Hoberman and Garfinkel (1988) found only three percent of their cohort under the age of 15, and Thompson (1987) reported only seven percent of his sample aged 14 and under. Suicide rates among 10 to 14 years olds increased relatively little between 1960 and 1981 (Hawton, 1986); however, between 1980 and 1985, the rate for this age group doubled (C.D.C., 1987).

Youthful suicide victims are predominantly male; in 1980, for middle adolescents, the rate for males was nearly five times relative to females (C.D.C., 1986); this is in contrast with suicide attempts, where females greatly exceed males (Hawton, 1986). Moreover, the rate of suicide between 1950 and 1980 has increased more for males (295%) than for females (67%) (C.D.C., 1986).

Marked racial differences also characterize youth suicide victims in the United States, with Caucasians committing suicide at twice the rate than most minority youth (C.D.C, 1986). However, suicide rates are especially high among certain tribes of Native Americans; among 15 to 24 year olds, the rate is five times greater than the general population of adolescents and young adults (U.S. Department of Health, Education and Welfare, 1973).

According to Hawton (1986), suicides are more common among married than single adolescents. Hoberman and Garfinkel (1988) found only two percent of their adolescent decedents were married, with 80% living with their parents. Regarding occupation, this study also found that most adolescent suicide victims were students. Of the remainder, 16% were working in blue collar jobs, with nine percent in other positions while four percent were unemployed. It is worth noting that in the United States, university students, including those attending more competitive schools, are not at elevated risk for suicide; however, in the United Kingdom, such students are at greater risk (Eisenberg, 1980; Hawton, 1986).

METHODS OF DEATH

Firearms are the major means of suicide among young suicides. According to the C.D.C. (1986), between 1970 and 1980, 60% of suicides between the ages of 15 and 19 involved guns; the other methods of death were: hanging or suffocation (18%), ingestion

(10%); and poisoning by gas (7%). Suicide by firearms appears to be increasing faster than deaths through other means (C.D.C., 1986; Brent, Perper, & Allman, 1987). In addition, firearms are an especially common method of suicide when the decedent has consumed alcohol (Brent et al., 1987). In the studies of young suicides, various regional differences in the means of suicide are found. Thus, in Poteet's (1987) study in Tennessee, 74% of the deaths involved firearms, while Cosand et al., (1982), Garfinkel and Golombek (1983), and Hoberman and Garfinkel (1988) all showed firearms were involved approximately 45% of the time. This last study also found an excess of deaths from carbon monoxide poisoning. In addition, Hoberman and Garfinkel (1988) noted that 38% of fatal overdoses involved prescribed anti-depressants, while 24% were from analgesics. It is worth noting that despite studies which examined potential misclassifications of suicides as accidents very few young suicides involve motor vehicle accidents (Brent et al., 1987; Hoberman & Garfinkel, 1988). Similarly, Schmidt, Perlin, Townes, Fisher, and Schaffer (1972) in a study of 111 single vehicle fatalities identified only three percent as suicides. The choice of a particular method of suicide probably reflects the availability of that means. Thompson (1987) found that rural and Native American suicides were much more likely to involve a firearm; among both those populations, guns were more commonly available than among urban persons. Brent et al., (1988) showed that firearms were more likely to have been present in the homes of suicide completers than a control group of suicidal ideators and attempters.

As might be expected, there are sex differences in the methods of suicide. Nationally, of youthful suicides, 62% of males employed firearms compared to 48% of females; males were also more likely to hang themselves (20%), while females were more likely to die from self-poisoning (28%) (C.D.C., 1986). However, Hoberman and Garfinkel (1988) showed that males who died from overdoses were more likely to take prescribed anti-depressants while females tended to ingest analgesics and other pharmacological agents. In addition, data from the C.D.C. (1986) indicates that, nationally, increasing numbers of suicides by young females involve the use of firearms, while decreasing numbers of this group die as a result of drug overdoses.

The method of suicide is also affected by age differences. Both Schaffer (1974) and Hoberman and Garfinkel (1988) found that younger suicides were much more likely to die from hanging, while firearms and carbon monoxide poisoning were more common for older suicides.

CIRCUMSTANCES OF THE SUICIDAL ACT

Most suicides among children and adolescents occur in their home (Garfinkel & Golombek, 1983; Hoberman & Garfinkel, 1988). Hoberman and Garfinkel (1988) collected data on circumstances of the suicide. They noted that someone else was present at the time of death 30% of the time, while in another 29% of cases, contact with the decedent was imminent. Only 29% of the decedents appeared to have taken active precautions against discovery. However, Brent et al. (1988) found more evidence of such precautions and planning. Suicidal individuals often remark about suicide prior to their death, especially females, but often those remarks are quite proximal to the suicide (Hoberman & Garfinkel, 1988). Schaffer (in Holden, 1986) reported that in his most recent psychological autopsy study of adolescent suicides, there was no evidence of a lengthy "brooding" period prior to the suicides. Poteet (1987) found that one-third of her subjects showed signs of depression at the time of their death. However, Hoberman and Garfinkel (1988) characterized nearly one-half of their subjects as sad or despairing, with another 20% viewed as angry. While older adolescents were more likely to be described as sad or despairing, younger suicides were much more likely to display anger prior to their suicide; Schaffer (1974) reported that 23% of his younger group of suicides left hostile suicide notes. Studies indicate some variation regarding suicide notes. Both Schaffer (1974) and Hoberman and Garfinkel (1988) reported such notes were left close to half of the time, while in other reports, notes were present less than 30% of the time (e.g., Poteet, 1987; Thompson, 1987). This can be compared to adult suicides where approximately one-third of the decedents leave notes (Murphy, 1986). In a review of the content of suicide notes, Leenaars and Balance (1984), noted differences between younger and older individuals, youthful suicide notes were more harshly self-critical and reflected self-perceptions of worthlessness. Poteet (1987) reported that of the notes left by her sample of suicides, themes of hopelessness and that life was not worth living were evident.

Intoxication is an important factor in young suicides. Research has demonstrated that, particularly in the United Sates, rates of suicide are higher in states where alcohol consumption is higher (Lester, 1980). Poteet (1987), Brent et al., (1987) and Hoberman and Garfinkel (1988) demonstrated that at least 45% of the decedents in their studies showed evidence of alcohol or drug use at the actual time of death; in the last study, blood alcohol levels were as high as .30 meq/L. Similarly, a report from the Los Angeles Suicide Prevention Center (Peck, 1984) reported that as many as 40-50% of adolescent and college-aged suicides were abusing alcohol and/or drugs at the time of their death. Moreover, according to Brent et al., the rate of adolescent suicides with a positive blood alcohol concentration increased fourfold between 1968 and 1983. This study also indicated a direct relationship between both a positive blood alcohol concentration (BAC) and a state of intoxication (e.g., BAC > 0.1%) and the use of firearms as the means of death. They also found that drug positive suicide victims were more likely to have died of drug overdoses.

Evidence for the seasonality of adolescent suicide has varied. Both Garfinkel and Golombek (1983) and Thompson (1987) reported an increase in youth suicide in the fall of the year. In contrast, Hoberman and Garfinkel (1988) showed a constant rate of death throughout the entire year.

PSYCHIATRIC DISORDERS

The relationship between psychiatric disorders and youthful suicide has been a matter of some controversy. Much of the earlier discussions of young suicide suggested that psychiatric disorders played relatively little role in such suicides; these acts were said to "have appeared out of nowhere." This was marked in contrast to the findings for adult suicides, where almost all adult suicides had experienced psychiatric episodes, predominantly affective disorders and alcohol abuse (e.g., Robbins, Murphy, Wilkinson, Gassner &

Kayes, 1959; Dorpat & Ripley, 1960; and Barraclough, Bunch, Nelson & Sainsbury, 1974).

Garfinkel and Golombek (1983), in an archival study, identified treated psychiatric disorder in 25% of their sample (mostly depressive disorders). Other studies of youthful suicide present evidence of rates of psychiatric disorders at least twice as high. Cosand et al. (1982) found evidence of "emotional instability" in 35% of their sample; more than 60% were said to be "despondent" at the time of their death. Overall, this study concluded that "evidence of pre-suicide psychological problems were pronounced" (p. 926). Schaffer (1974) found that only 13% of his subjects did not show affective or anti-social symptoms and nearly 60% of his sample demonstrated a combination of antisocial and affective symptoms. Poteet (1987) indicated that 28% of the decedents in her study showed evidence of alcohol or substance abuse and 33% showed signs of depression or "mental problems." Shaffi and associates (1985) demonstrated high rates of several psychiatric disorders in their sample of suicide completers: 76% were depressed, 70% were alcohol or substance abusers, and 70% had symptoms of anti-social behavior. Schaffer (1985; in Holden, 1986) reported that approximately 2/3 of his sample of adolescent suicides were characterized by anti-social behavior or alcohol or drug abuse, while only 30% showed evidence of depression. In addition, this investigation found high rates of eating disorders among female decedents. Thompson (1987) found that 33% of his sample were alcoholic while 17% were characterized by substance abuse. Hoberman and Garfinkel (1988) reported that 50% of the suicide victims showed clear evidence of one or multiple psychiatric disorders, mostly depressive disorders or alcohol or substance abuse disorders. Moreover, most of these disorders appeared to be of a chronic nature, as opposed to more acute conditions. Affective disorder, in general, were more likely to characterize females who committed suicide. Older adolescents were also more likely to have affective disorders, while younger suicides were more likely to display anti-social behavior. Rich, Young and Fowler (1986) indicated that drug abuse diagnoses were strongly associated with suicides (70%) in persons under 30.

Brent et al. (1988) have presented the most detailed description of the psychiatric disorders of youthful completed suicide victims. They found that 93% of their sample had at least one major psychiatric diagnosis by parental report. Affective disorders were the most common type of psychiatric disorder at the time of their death; 41% were diagnosed as having a major depressive disorder; 22% were rated as having a dysthymic disorder; and 7% were seen as experiencing a manic or hypomanic episode. Other common diagnoses at the time of death were as follows: substance abuse (41%); attention deficit disorder (26%); conduct disorder (22%); and overanxious disorder (15%). Moreover, young suicide completers were more likely than a control group of suicide attempters to be characterized by psychiatric co-morbidity — e.g., having an affective disorder and another disorder; this was especially true for those decedents with bipolar illness. Regarding lifetime psychiatric diagnoses, two-thirds were rated as having experienced some type of affective disorder; 11% had recurrent unipolar depression and 22% had bipolar affective disorder. The average age onset for a first psychiatric episode was 10 to 11 years and 80% had episodes of psychiatric illness prior to the episode at the time of their death. Overall, then, younger suicides resemble older suicides in both the incidence and type of psychiatric disorders they experience. Such disorders typically involve affective distress and dysfunctional thinking. Thus as Murphy (1986) notes:

> The fabled "rational" suicide — carefully considered self-destruction undertaken for personal reasons unattended by psychiatric illness — is largely a myth. (p.563)

The relationship between completed suicide, a history of suicidal ideation and attempts is not firmly established in this age group. Unfortunately, few long-term follow-up studies of adolescent suicide attempters have been conducted. Goldacre and Hawton (1985) examined the outcome over a three year period for 2,492 persons aged 12 to 20 years who overdosed and had been seen for evaluation; only six of these individuals committed suicide. Thus, less than one percent of this group eventually became suicide victims. Garfinkel, Froese and Hood (1982) found slightly more than a 2% death rate in a group of 505 young adolescent attempters. Thompson (1987) and Hoberman and Garfinkel (1988) identified prior suicide attempts in 10% and 20% respectively of their samples. Poteet (1987) showed that 29% of her sample had previously displayed suicidal intent or made a suicide attempt while 35% of another sample had made prior attempts (Cosand et al., 1982). Schaffer (1974) indicated suicide threats, mention of suicide, or previous suicidal behavior in 40% of his sample, most of the time within 24 hours of the actual death. In their study, Brent et al. (1988) indicated that 26% of the suicide victims had made suicide threats and 22% suicide attempts prior to their deaths. Typically, threats were made proximal of their death and in 50% were shared only with a peer or sibling. Only Shaffi et al., (1985) have reported high rates of prior suicidal behavior in a sample of suicide completers. They found that 55% of their sample verbalized a suicide threat, while 40% had made a suicide attempt. The available evidence, therefore, suggests an important, but hardly universal association between completed suicide and previous suicidal attempts. Most studies indicate that females who die are approximately twice as likely to have made at least one prior suicide attempt (Thompson, 1987; Hoberman & Garfinkel, 1988).

Given the high rates of psychiatric disorders which characterize young suicide completers, their use of mental health services becomes of interest. While Thompson (1987) showed that 28% of his sample of suicides had previous psychiatric contact, Cosand, Bourque and Kraus (182) noted that only 17% of suicide victims in their study had ever received psychiatric treatment. Schaffer (1974) reported that 30% of his sample was receiving or awaiting treatment at the time of their death. Forty-five percent of the decedents in Shaffi et al., (1985) had received previous psychiatric treatment. Brent et al., (1988) found that one-third of the suicide victims studied had one or more psychiatric contacts, however, only 2/27 were receiving treatment at the time of their death. In one report, female decedents were four times as likely to have a history of prior psychiatric contact (Thompson, 1987). However, another study (Cosand et al., 1982) indicated that in the most recent birth cohort, nearly half of the male suicides had a history of psychiatric treatment.

PRECIPITANTS

Most children and adolescents who suicide do so after experiencing some type of stressor. Ninety percent of Schaffer's (1974) and 64% of Poteet's samples were identified as encountering a negative event prior to their deaths; similarly, Hoberman and Garfinkel (1988) identified a precipitant to suicide in the great majority of the youthful suicides in their study. In Thompson's (1987) investigation, the rates for stressors were as follows: relationship breakups (26%); family disputes (22%); and legal problems (16%). Hoberman and Garfinkel (1988) noted the following incidence of precipitants: arguments (19%); school problems (14%); disappointments (11%); difficulties with the police (10%); separations or threat of separations (8%); relationship break-up (5%); and problems at work (5%). Brent et al. (1988) found that interpersonal conflict occurred prior to 70% of young suicides; seventy percent of these youth were also likely to have experienced an external stressor, predominantly school problems, legal difficulties, and financial problems. A study of youthful suicide completers (persons under the age of 30) noted very high rates of interpersonal conflict loss, economic problems, and legal difficulties (Rich, Fowler, Fogarty & Young, 1988). Pettifor et al., (1983) identified high rates of school problems in their sample of suicides. Arguments, the most common precipitant, Hoberman and Garfinkel (1988) noted tended to occur within twelve hours of the suicide and concerned a variety of subjects: drug use; discipline practices; academic performance; and dating. Arguments were typically with a girlfriend or with a parent; in the latter case, they were more likely to be with a parent of the same sex as the decedent. Generally, precipitants occurred within 24 hours preceding the suicide. While few sex differences were identified in the types of precipitants, both pregnancy and a recent physical or sexual assault were more common in female suicide victims. The association between being victimized and suicide agrees with Robbins' finding (in Holden, 1986) that being assaulted is strongly predictive of suicidal behavior. Male completers were much more likely to have been arrested or to have had "legal problems" in two investigations (Cosand et al., 1982; Thompson, 1987) but another study found no such gender difference (Hoberman & Garfinkel, 1988). Age differences were evident for precipitants for suicides. Hoberman and Garfinkel (1988) found that suicides of persons 14 and under were twice as likely to be precipitated by school problems; similarly, the most common stressor in Schaffer's (1974) sample of younger suicides was a disciplinary crisis, usually related to school behavior.

BEHAVIORAL CHARACTERISTICS

Hoberman and Garfinkel (1988) did not find a single personality descriptor applicable to more than 18% of their sample. The most common descriptive categories were those suggestive of being withdrawn, lonely, or hypersensitive. Schaffer (1974) identified 30% of his sample as being hypersensitive, 30% as withdrawn or uncommunicative, and 20% as impulsive; characteristics that tended to overlap individuals. Shaffi and associates demonstrated that 70% of their sample were rated as having "inhibited personalities," defined by withdrawal and extreme sensitivity. The presence of extreme sensitivity suggests that such adolescents may experience relatively extreme emotional reactions to events and/or may have difficulty modulating or regulating those reactions. Their social withdrawal indicates that, in general, they are uncomfortable with other persons and may be deficient in social skills. Particularly under conditions of stress, they may isolate further, rather than attempting or being able to solicit social support to mediate their distress or obtain assistance in resolving a problematic situation.

An early study of college-aged suicide completers showed a pattern of progressive social withdrawal and isolation dating back to early adolescence (Peck and Schrut, 1971). According to Hoberman and Garfinkel (1988), the majority of youthful suicides, especially males, were described as poor students. In addition, 76% of the cases, the decedent's academic performance had changed for the worse in the previous year. Pettifor et al. (1983) also noted lower grades in school a well as more negative attitudes towards school and teachers. Schaffer (1985) reported that his sample of adolescent suicides were generally characterized as having a low or borderline intellectual development; decedents tended to show impaired reading ability and a history of school failures.

While Garfinkel and Golombek (1983) found 5% of their sample had a physical illness for which they were being treated, a later study (Hoberman & Garfinkel, 1988) noted that 31% of the suicide victims were described as being in good health; chronic illnesses, physical disabilities, and a variety of more acute illnesses and physical complaints were common. Cosand and associates (1982) showed that the association of physical illness and suicide increased with the age of the decedent.

Early discussions of the families of youthful suicide victims tended to minimize the likelihood of dysfunction. However, increasing evidence demonstrates that a variety of family problems are quite common in these families. In Schaffer's (1974) study, 23% of the decedents came from homes where divorce had occurred; within four years of the suicide, another 20% of these parents had divorced. The study by Pettifor et al. found higher rates of residential change and a greater number of parent-child separations in their study. Overall, parent-child support was described as poor. Siblings in these families were also noted to have a greater number and range of problems. Shaffi et al. (1985) characterized 55% of the families of decedents as being either physically or emotionally abusive or marked by parental absence. Another report on suicide completers (Peck, 1984), found that nearly two-thirds of suicide victims were not on good terms with their family; approximately 90% thought that their family did not understand them. Additionally, another 42% reported physical fights with family members.

Families of suicide victims also evidence higher rates of psychiatric disorders. As many as half of the families in Schaffer's (1974) study had consulted someone for "emotional symptoms." In these families, rates of depression (20%), anxiety (10%) and psychotic symptoms (10%) were high; 26% of the parents were described as heavy drinkers. Thirteen percent of these families had a parent or sibling attempt suicide before the child's death. Similarly, 60% of the parents in the Shaffi's et al., (1985) sample were viewed as having "emotional problems." Brent et al. (1988) observed the most detailed analysis of the types of psychiatric disorders found in the families of youthful suicide completers. Rates of major depressive disorder, bipolar disorder, anti-social personality disorder, and completed suicide were elevated, while rates of alcohol and drug abuse were comparable, relative to national prevalence data.

Other evidence exists that there may be a genetic contribution to suicide. Schulsinger, Kety, Rosenthal, and Wender (1979), in a study of children adopted early in life, present evidence that completed suicides were more strongly related to suicide in biological as opposed to adoptive relatives. Similarly, Egeland and Sussex (1985) demonstrated that suicides clustered in particular family pedigrees.

EXPOSURE TO SUICIDE

Evidence is accumulating that exposure to the notion of suicide has an impact on adolescent suicide completions. Such adolescents are more likely to have been exposed to suicidal behavior by a friend or family member (65%) compared to a control group (18%) (Shaffi et al., 1985). As noted previously, both Schaffer (1974) and Brent et al., (1988) showed elevated rates of suicidal behavioral among families of suicide completers. Bollen and Phillips (1982) observed that suicide rates vary with media coverage so that front-page display of news of a suicide will have a temporary effect of increasing rates of suicide within the area of exposure. Phillips and Carstensen (1986) demonstrated an excess of suicides after nationally televised news or feature stories about suicide, with a greater increase for more extensive coverage. They also found that adolescent suicides were more likely than adult suicides to increase after stories about suicide. In addition, they showed that this effect was not simply that of provoking a suicide that would have occurred later in a given time period as there was no compensatory decline later in time.

Gould and Schaffer (1986) found that the number of completed and attempted suicides in adolescents was higher than would have been predicted after fictional television movies about suicide were aired. In each of these studies, the authors concluded that the evidence was suggestive that some adolescent suicides are the result of imitation. Davison and Gould (1986) have theorized about several factors which might mediate the degree of contagion: the general vulnerability of a youth; the direct or indirect means of transmission regarding information about a suicide; the relative influence of a suicide role model; and the relative "dosage" of exposure to information concerning one or more suicides.

Well-known clusters of adolescent suicides include those in Plano, Texas; Westchester and Rockland counties in New York; and Omaha, Nebraska. Another example of the effects of imitation centered around the group suicide of four New Jersey adolescents in 1987 by carbon monoxide poisoning in an underground garage. Within days of the extensive publicity surrounding the suicides, two adolescents in Chicago committed suicide in the same manner; within several weeks, two adolescents attempted suicide in the same manner in the same garage as the original four suicides. Clearly, the evidence is supportive of the notion that well-publicized reports of suicides and suicidal behavior in a family member or peer may provide a model for suicide among young persons. The effects of imitation are perhaps best seen in the instance of suicide clusters.

INTEGRATION OF RESEARCH FINDINGS

Suicide is primarily an act of white males and its frequency increases with age. As with adult suicide, psychiatric disorders appear to be the most significant precondition to youth suicide; most young persons who commit suicide are experiencing an episode of a psychiatric disorder. These disorders are generally of long duration episodic or are chronic in nature. Conduct disorders appear to be strongly related to suicide in children and younger adolescents; it is likely that the social consequences of such behavior become more severe with increasing age. More generally, affective disorders, alcohol and substance abuse demonstrate a particular relationship to suicide in the young as they do in older suicides. Moreover, the incidence of these types of disorders increase during the adolescent years. Each of these disorders is associated with a greater likelihood of suicidal thinking (Brent, Kalas, Edelbrock, Costell, & Dulcan, 1986). Thus, 76% of a community sample of depressed adolescents reported thinking about suicide compared to only 18% of non-depressed adolescents (Hoberman, Garfinkel, Parsons & Walker, 1986). Moreover, 27% of these depressed adolescents reported suicide attempts within the last month; only one percent of their non-depressed peers indicated a recent attempt. As this review demonstrates, about 30% of suicide completers have a history of previous suicidal ideation or suicide attempts. Pettifor et al., (1983) found that the existence of life threatening thoughts and behavior was the variable which best distinguished between young suicide completers and a psychiatric control group. Some continuum of suicidality seems evident: suicidal ideation is associated with a higher likelihood of suicide attempts and a history of such attempts is related to a greater likelihood of suicide completions among young persons.

At the same time, most depressed or substance-abusing young people neither attempt nor complete suicide; even the great majority of attempters do not proceed to take their lives. Furthermore, the incidence of depression is twice as great for females than for males, while the ratio of suicide attempters is 3:1 female to male; while males complete suicide more often. Thus, it seems other characteristics *must* exist which differentiate those youth with psychiatric disorders who are at risk for suicide from those who are not. Schaffer (Holden, 1986) has argued that boys may be at greater risk simply as a result of their comfort with and the relative availability of firearms. Certainly, the study by Brent et al., (1988) indicates the significance of the availability and proximity of a firearm in differentiating between those who attempt and complete suicide. Males, as a group, may be more prone to impulsivity and emotional explosiveness. It is noteworthy that in this and Schaffer's (1974) study, that the youngest suicides are more likely to be angry, aggressive, antisocial males. Additionally, a state of hopelessness has been shown to be an accurate predictor of eventual suicide (within five to ten years) in a sample of psychiatric patients reporting suicidal ideation (Beck, Steer, Kovacs, & Garrison, 1985). This finding suggests that despair or pessimism may be an important mediator between psychiatric disorder and suicide. Factors which may be related to such hopelessness include the chronicity of disorder, the failure to identify the presence of psychiatric disorders, the relative lack of treatment for those disorders, inadequate treatment of those disorders, or the tendency of disorders to elicit stressors.

The circumstances of young suicide also bear consideration. Precipitants appear to precede most suicides; yet these stressors generally appear to be the same type of life events which occur for most adolescents (Hoberman, Garfinkel, Parsons & Walker, 1986).

Stressors alone, do not likely pose a risk for the average adolescent. Instead, it appears to be the existence of stressors for particular individuals with pre-existing psychiatric conditions that creates a climate of risk. Some of the stressors may be a consequence of being depressed, or abusing substances and may not be independently occurring traumatic life events. Boys appear to be more affected by arguments in significant relationships and relationship breakups. The greater degree of distress experienced by males after relationship breakups was demonstrated in a study of dating couples by Hill, Peplau and Rubin (1976). Girls' suicides show an increasing association with assaults. Given the alarming high rate of sexual assaults experienced by adolescent females (e.g., Koss, Gidycz & Wisniewski, 1987), this becomes an especially significant finding.

The seemingly impulsive, crisis-nature of the actual suicide is impressive. Relatively few suicides showed evidence of advance planning or even precautions against being stopped or discovered at the time of the act. Additionally, the extent and degree of intoxication prior to death suggests a mental state of impaired judgement; it raises questions about the capacity for these young people to make rational judgments about their current life circumstances.

Finally, it is worth considering the effect of the increasing amount of attention society provides for suicide among the young. Suicide rates tend to correlate with the degree of social acceptance of suicidal behavior in particular cultures and sub-cultures (Hawton, 1986). It is quite likely that the heightened exposure in the media and in schools of both incidents and concerns about adolescent suicide is a double-edged sword. While it may increase sensitivity and responsiveness to a distressed adolescent, it may also serve to increase the acceptance and thereby the likelihood of suicide as an option of life's difficulties among such adolescents.

Overall then, the picture of the adolescent at risk for completed suicide is one of a young person with multiple problems and a limited and maladaptive repertoire of coping skills. As can be seen in Figure 1, more long-standing conditions of psychiatric disorders, family discord, deficits in affect and impulse management, social skills, and problem-solving skills are all potential vulnerabilities which interact with immediate stressors to elicit a state of emotional distress. In the absence of effective attempts to resolve the current crisis, hopelessness ensues. The availability of reason-impairing al-

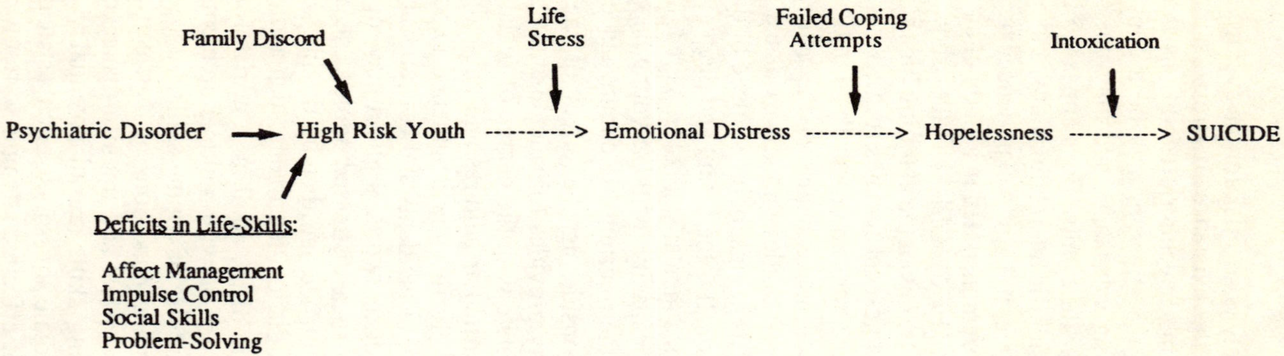

THE PATHWAY FROM RISK FACTORS TO COMPLETED SUICIDE

Figure 1

cohol or drugs, and the presence of life-threatening agents are the final links in the pathway towards completed suicide.

ADOLESCENCE AS A TIME OF RISK FOR SUICIDE

Schaffer and Fisher (1981) have suggested a number of factors which may protect children from suicide including lower rates of psychiatric disorders, the greater availability of social and emotional support from families, and their lack of cognitive maturity, characterized by a lack of abstract thinking. In contrast, a number of characteristics of adolescents as a particular developmental time period suggest reasons why youth may become more vulnerable to commit suicide. Despite popular notions of adolescence as a universal time of great psychological and social upheaval, recent investigations have demonstrated that the majority of adolescents are not in the constant throes of turmoil (Rutter, Graham, Chadwick & Yule, 1976; Offer, Ostrov & Howard, 1984). Nonetheless, adolescence is a period of assimilating and accommodating to a variety of changes. Adolescents must deal with dramatic changes in their physical appearance; moreover, physical maturation occurs at increasingly younger ages. These changes have the potential to elicit marked demands on a youth's self-concept as well as changes in social definitions and the behavior of significant others. An adolescent must contend with intensified drives and affective experiences, and often a decreased tolerance for the frustration of needs; additionally, physical maturation and growth create an increased capacity for action and reaction. Thus, Rutter et al., (1976) have demonstrated a linear increase in the experience of depression as a function of making the transition from prepubertal to postpubertal status. Cognitively, many adolescents are in transition between concrete, present-oriented thought and the capacity for abstract, hypothetical thought; they cannot fully consider all of the probable consequences of their actions nor fully understand the feelings or behavior of others. As they acquire the possibility of more abstract and hypothetical thought, adolescents are better able to make comparisons between their life situation and that of others and to imagine the possibility of other, better life circumstances. The increasing but still limited ability to contemplate the future, may encourage them to believe that problematic circumstances may be permanent.

Moreover, an adolescent must come to terms with an increased self-consciousness and capacity for self- and other-evaluation as well as the realization that personal expectations and fantasies must be tempered with the realities of one's actual abilities and expectations. Adolescence is a time of reconciling a need for autonomy and intimacy in peer relations with the previous reliance on family for affirmation and need gratification. Consequently, the typical adolescent is in the midst of a change in social support, so that neither family or peers provide complete acceptance or validation; in turn, this makes it difficult for the youth to determine what is normative for this stage of life and to find comfort in one's anxiety and distress. Finally, adolescence is a time of self-definition; a youth feels pressed to integrate the aforementioned changes with previous values and experiences and to organize them into a personal identity which defines his or her self as a stable, differentiated entity. Overall, adolescence is a time of multiple transitions, and thus of great ambiguity and uncertainty—quite different from the concrete, limited, and more predictable world of the younger child. Consequently, it appears to be a period of increased risk for psychiatric disorder and suicidal ideation and behavior.

ACCOUNTING FOR THE RISE IN YOUTHFUL SUICIDES

It is unlikely that any single factor can be viewed as responsible for the increasing rates of suicide completions among the young. Rather, multiple factors may be converging to heighten the risk of such behavior among the young. To begin with, the nature of the family has changed markedly in recent years. Less than 10% of American families, include two parents where one parent is a full-time homemaker. Divorce effects a great number of homes, with the rate of more than doubling between 1954 and 1978 (Stack, 1986); nearly half of all children spend time in a home with a single-parent. In most families, both parents work. Overall, then, children have less parental involvement and support; many have experienced interpersonal strife and a wide range of disruptions, including changes in financial status, residence and schools. Average family income has shown a relative decline over the last thirty years; increasing numbers of children grow up in poverty. Increased mobility also means less contact with extended family. Further, involvement with organized religion has declined parallel to the rise in suicide rates (Stack, 1986). These trends suggest that children and adolescents have even less social support immediately available to them.

In addition, authorities have suggested a number of changes in behavior and values which may have important implications for the rise in psychiatric disorders and general demoralization among the young. Elkind (1981) called attention to the "hurried child" phenomenon whereby children are pressured to pursue intense early preparation or training to maximize academic, athletic, and artistic success. In addition, it is worth noting that adolescents are faced with a variety of decisions regarding sexual behavior and identity, alcohol and drug use, and educational or career paths at earlier ages. Winn (1983) has described the "adultification" of youth; the early and intense exposure to the young to themes of explicit sexuality, violence, and issues of unethical behavior. In addition, she has noted the increasing tendency of parents to abdicate to their children's demands for greater autonomy at earlier ages. Winn and Elkind both raise questions about developmental inappropriateness of these different practices. Intense parental overinvolvement can compromise a child's ability to play and to develop their own set of interests and thereby a unique identity, while intense, ungraduated exposure to the problematic issues of the adult world can result in feelings of abandonment and a jaded, alienated stance to the world. Additionally, youth seem desensitized toward death, including suicide. Media experiences have exposed them to countless deaths, with suicide often portrayed in an inaccurate and romanticized manner. Suicide may have become an accepted solution to common difficulties. In addition, improvements in health care and the distance of family members have insulated adolescents from the painful emotional realities of death.

A variety of other trends also appear to characterize today's youth. There seems to be little tolerance for being average; rather, there is a sense that one's identity is predicated on being special or unique relative to peers. Many adolescents complain that they are "nobodies" because they are not special in some areas of their lives; as one suicide note explained "there is no room in this world for nobodies." Current social values emphasize that adolescents can be anything they want to be; it is an idealogy of unlimited opportunities. Media influences (e.g., television programs like Dallas or Dynasty) seem to encourage youth to desire and believe they can and should have lives of wealth and power. In fact, this is a generation of American youth who will likely have substantially more restricted economic opportunities than their parents. Thus, in adolescence, there may be an increasing collision between elevated expectations and the much more limited possibilities of their adult life; this may be especially painful for troubled youths, who have opted for short-term gratification (e.g., no homework) at the expense of longer-term goals (better school grades). Further, there is a tendency among contemporary youth to define their goals in life in material terms — if only they possess the socially appropriate "things" (e.g., cars, clothes) they will be fulfilled. This orientation appears to be at the expense of prizing close, intimate relationships. Rather, there is a tendency to see relationships as "things," and the sense that if one is not satisfied with relationships, one simply exchanges them for a more current and appropriate model. A possible consequence of the rapidly, technologically-sophisticated and comforted world is that adolescents have become accustomed to easy work.

Given the variety of psychological and social changes developmentally intrinsic to adolescence, the impact of the increasing demographic and sociocultural changes must be quite significant. A probable link between this host of demands, the accompanying conflicts, and suicide is in the likelihood of elevated rates of psychopathology. In fact, rates of depression and alcohol abuse have increased for recent cohorts of young persons (respectively, Klerman, Lavori, Rice, Reich, Endicott, Andreason, Keller, Hirschfield, 1985; Macdonald, 1987). In addition, while no definitive data on increased rates of anti-social behavior is available, Kazdin (1987) has described the extremely high rates of anti-social behavior among young persons. Thus, the increase in several inter-related psychiatric disorders is probably the central agent driving the rising rate of suicides in young persons. Moreover, this increase in the experience of psychiatric disorders must be considered in the context of the changes in the structure of the family. While these changes may well be contributory of the disorders in the first place, they may also have a significant effect on the identification and response to those disorders. Increasingly stressed parents, themselves often suffering from psychiatric disorders, with decreasing time to interact with their children, may not recognize the distress of their children, may fail to acknowledge its presence or severity, or may simply not be able to provide the emotional reassurance and support their dysfunctional children require.

IMPLICATIONS FOR SUICIDE PREVENTION

Several studies have demonstrated that suicide prevention programs have not made a significant impact on the rate of suicides (Bridge, Potkin, Sung & Woldo, 1977; Barraclough, Jennings & Moss, 1978; and Miller, Coombs, Mukherjee & Barton, 1979). In recent years, a number of suicide prevention curricula have been developed specifically targeted at youth. Garfinkel (1986) has noted that many of these curricula focus to a great degree on the circumstances surrounding suicides and tend to deemphasize the relationship between psychopathology and suicide. It is apparent that a focus on precipitants, signs of premeditation or planning is likely to be unproductive given the normative nature of the stresses experienced by young suicides and the apparently impulsive nature of the actual suicidal act. The likelihood of preventing particular suicides at the time of the act seems low.

The emphasis in youth suicide prevention programs must be on the early identification and appropriate treatment of the episodes of psychopathology which underlie and precede most instances of suicide in young persons. A number of studies have demonstrated that parents (Leon, Kendall, & Garber, 1980; Weisman, Orvaschel, & Padian, 1980) or teachers (Lefkowitz & Tesiny, 1984; Sacco & Graves, 1985) are generally inaccurate judges of the presence of depression in children or adolescents. Murphy (1975) has shown that physicians often fail to identify depression in patients who eventually suicide and fail to inquire about suicidality, even when they recognize that a patient is dysphoric or demoralized. Additionally, peers or siblings are often the person most likely to be informed of suicidal ideation or threats (Brent et al., 1988). Yet research indicates that peers so informed often respond in inappropriate ways to the possibility of suicide by failing to inform others to allow for intervention (Mishara, 1982). To contain the rising rates of adolescent suicide, programs are needed to train parents, teachers, physicians, and peers to recognize depressive disorders, alcohol and substance abuse in adolescents, and make appropriate referrals. Each of these groups must be encouraged to understand the circumstances of risk for vulnerable youth and to seek professional assistance in evaluating the potential suicidality of a given young person. Khuri and Akiskal (1983) have made a strong argument that energetic treatment and ongoing follow-up of patients with primary and secondary affective disorders will prove to be an effective method of preventing suicide. The most effective treatment for youth who are at elevated risk for suicide is a combination of multi-dimensional counseling and appropriately administered medication. The targets of intervention are indicated by the characteristics of the at-risk youth: containing or reducing psychiatric symptomatology; increasing the ability to modulate affective distress and impulsivity, reducing conflict in and facilitating the utilization of social relationships for support; to effectively problem-solve; and to change dysfunctional family patterns. However, considerably more research is needed to better understand the most effective treatment for adolescents experiencing affective disorders or alcohol and substance abuse.

The increasing rates of psychiatric disorders also suggest that children and adolescents in general might benefit greatly from specific instruction in coping skills as part of their regular education. In addition, efforts should be directed toward reducing more intensive assistance to adolescents who encounter demanding stressors and toward reducing the nature and degree of publicity provided for suicide. In particular, attempts should be made both to desensationalize and deromanticize suicide; in fact, given the public concern about adolescent suicide, it makes sense that the selection of suicide as a response to life difficulties be stigmatized to some degree to reduce the possibility of positive identification or modeling by others. Efforts at decreasing the availability of quick-acting methods of death, especially firearms, may also help to contain the rate of suicide among young. In closing, the results of this review suggest that youth at risk for completed suicide are males who have either an affective disorder or alcohol or drug abuse in the context of familial dysfunction and maladaptive coping mechanisms and who have experienced an acute, proximal stressor which involves either a social loss or a blow to their self-esteem. Such information can begin to provide the foundation of realistic and effective strategies to reduce the rates of youth who tragically take their lives in an impulsive desire to manage the acute distress of their psychiatric disorders.

BIBLIOGRAPHY

Barraclough, B.M., Bunch, J., Nelson, B. & Sainsbury, P. (1974). A hundred cases of suicide: Clinical aspects. *Br J Psychol, 125*:355-373.

Barraclough, B.M., Jennings, C. & Moss, J.R. (1978). Suicide prevention by the Samaritian: A controlled study of effectiveness. *Lancet, 2*:868-870.

Beck, A.T., Steer, R.A. Kovacs, M. & Garrison, D. (1985). Hopelessness and eventual suicide: A 10-year prospective study of patients hospitalized with suicidal ideation. *Am J Psychiatry, 142*:559-563.

Berman, A. & Cohen-Sandler, R. (1982). Childhood and adolescent suicide research: A critique. *Crisis*, 3-5.

Blum, R. (1987). Contemporary threats to adolescent health in the United States. *JAMA, 257*:3390-3395.

Bollen, K.A. & Phillips, D.P. (1982). Imitative suicides: A national study of the effects of television news stories. *American Sociological Review, 47*:802-809.

Brent, D.A. Kalas, R., Edelbrock, C., Costello, A.J., Dulcan, M.K. & Conover, N. (1986). Psychopathology and its relationship to suicidal ideation in childhood and adolescence. *J Am. Acad Psychiatry, 25*:666-673.

Brent, D.A., Perper, J.A. & Allman, C.J. (1987). Alcoholism, firearms, and suicide among youth. *JAMA, 257*:3369-3372.

Brent, D.A., Perper, J.A., Goldstein, C.E., Cole, D.J., Allan, M.J., Allman, C.J. & Zelenak, J.P. (1988). Risk Factors for Adolescent Suicide. *Archives of General Psychiatry, 45*:581-588.

Bridge, T.P. Potkin, S.D., Sung, W.W.A. & Soldo, B.J. (1977). Suicide prevention centers. *J Nerv Ment Dis, 164*:18-24.

Centers for Disease Control (1986). *Youth Suicide in the United States*, 1970-1980.

Centers for Disease Control (1987). Death Rates for 282 Selected Causes of Death in the United States (1979-1985).

Cosand, Bourque & Krauss (1982).

Cosand, B.J., Bourque & Krauss, J.F. (1982). Suicide among adolescents in Sacramento County, California, 1950-1979. *Adolescence*, 17, 917-930.

Davidson, L. & Gould, M.S. (1986). *Contagion as a risk factor for youth suicide*. Paper presented for the Task Force on Youth Suicide, Work Group on Risk Factors, Department of Health and Human Services, April 30, 1986.

Dorpat, T.L. & Ripley, H.S. (1960). A study of suicide in the Seattle area. *Compr Psychiatry, 1*:349-359.

Egeland, J.A. & Sussex, J.N. (1985). Suicide and family loading for affective disorders. *JAMA*, *254*:915-918.

Eisenberg, L. (1980). Adolescent suicide: On taking arms against a sea of troubles. *Pediatrics*, *66*:315-320.

Elkind, D. (1981). *The Hurried Child*. Reading, Mass. Madison-Westley.

Fowler, R.C., Rich, L.L. & Young, D. (1986). San Diego Suicide Study II. Substance abuse in young cases. *Archives of General Psychiatry*, 43, 962-965.

Garfinkel, B.D. (1986). *School-Based Prevention Programs*. Paper presented at the National Conference on Prevention and Interventions in Youth Suicide, Oakland, California.

Garfinkel, B.D. & Golombek, H. (1983). Suicidal behavior in adolescents. In: *The Adolescent and Mood Disturbance*, ed. B.D. Garfinkel & H. Golombek. New York: International University Press, 189-217.

Garfinkel, B.D., Froese, A. & Hood, J. (1982). Suicide attempts in children and adolescents. *Am J Psychiatry*, *139*:1257-1261.

Goldacre, M. & Hawton, K. (1985). Repetition of self-poisoning and subsequent death in adolescents who take overdoses. *Br J Psychiatry*, *146*:395-398.

Gould, M.S. & Schaffer, D. (1986). The impact of suicide in television movies: Evidence of imitation. *N Engl J Med*, *315*:690-694.

Hawton, K. (1986). Suicide in adolescents. In: *Suicide*, Ed. A. Roy, Baltimore: Williams and Wilkins, pp. 135-150.

Hill, C., Rubin, Z. & Peplau, L. (1976). Breakups before marriage: The end of 103 affairs. *J Social Issues*, *33*:147-168.

Hoberman, H.M. & Garfinkel, B.D. (1988). Completed suicide in children and adolescents. *J Am Acad Child Adolesc Psychiatry*.

Hoberman, H.M., Garfinkel, B.D., Parsons, J.H. & Walker, J. (1986). *Epidemiology of depression in a community sample of high school students*. Paper presented at the American Academy of Child Psychiatry, Los Angeles, California, October.

Holden, C. (1986). Youth suicide: New research focuses on a growing social problem. *Science*, *233*:839-841.

Jan-Tausch, J. (1964). *Suicide in Children 1960-1963*. Trenton, New Jersey: New Jersey Public Schools, Department of Education.

Kazdin, A.E. (1987). Treatment of antisocial behavior in children: Current status of the future directions. *Psychol Bull*, *102*:187-203.

Khuri, R. & Akiskal, H.S. (1983). Suicide prevention: The necessity of treating contributory psychiatric disorders. *Psychiatr Clin North Am*, *6*:193-207.

Klerman, G.L., Lavori, P.W., Rice, J., Reich, T., Endicott, J., Andreason, N.C., Keller, M.B. & Hirschfield, R.M.A. (1985). Birth cohort trends and rates for major depressive disorder among relatives of patients with affective disorder. *Arch Gen Psychiatry*, *42*:689-695.

Koss, M.P., Gidycz, C.A. & Wisniewski, N. (1987). The scope of rape: Incidence and prevalence of sexual aggression and victimization in a national sample of higher education students. *J Consult Clin Psychol*, *55*(2):162-170.

Leenaars, A.A. & Balan, W.D.G. (1984). A predictive approach to suicide notes of young and old people from Freud's formulations with regard to suicide. *J Clin Psychol, 40*:1362-1364.

Lefkowitz, M.M. & Tesiny, E.P. (1980). Assessment of childhood depression. *J Consult Clin Psychol, 48*(1):43-50.

Leon, G.R. Kendall, P.C. & Garber, J. (1980). Depression in children: Parent, teacher, and child perspectives. *J Consult Clin Psychol, 8*:221-235.

Macdonald, D.I. (1987) Patterns of alcohol and drug use among adolescents. *Pediatr Clin North Am, 34*:275-288.

Miller, H.L., Coombs, D.W., Mukherjee, D. & Barton, S.N. (1979). Suicide prevention services in America. *Ala J Med Sci, 16*:26-31.

Mishara, B. (1982). College students' experiences with suicide and reactions to suicidal verbalizations: A model for prevention. *J Community Psychology, 10*:142-150.

Murphy, G.E. (1975). The physician's errors of omission. *Ann Intern Med, 82*:305-309.

Murphy, G.E. (1986). Suicide and Attempted Suicide. In: P.J. Clayton and G. Winokur (eds.) *The Medical Basis of Psychiatry*, Philadelphia: W.B. Saunders, 562-579.

Murphy, G.E. & Wetzel, R.D. (1980). Suicide risk by birth cohorts in the United States, 1949 to 1974. *Arch Gen Psychiatry, 37*:519-523.

Offer, D., Ostrov, E. & Howard, K.I. (1984). The self-image of normal adolescents. *New Dir Ment Health Serv, 22*:5-17.

Peck, M. (1984). Suicide in late adolescence and young adulthood. In: C.L. Hatton and S.M. Velenti (Eds.) *Suicide: Assessment and Intervention*. Norwalk, CT: Appleton-Century-Crofts, 220-230.

Peck, M.L. & Schrut, A. (1971). Suicidal behavior among college students. *HSMHA Health Reports, 86*, 149-156.

Pettifor, J., Perry, D., Plowman, B. & Pitcher, S. (1983). Risk factors predicting childhood and adolescent suicides: *J Child Care*.

Phillips, D.P. & Carstensen, L.L., (1986). Clustering of teenaged suicides after television news stories about suicide. *N Engl J Med, 315*:685-689.

Poteet, D.J. (1987). Adolescent suicide: A review of 87 cases of completed suicide in Shelby County, Tennessee. *Am J Forensic Med Pathol, 8*:12-17.

Rich, C.L., Fowler, R.C., Fogarty, L.A. & Young, D. (1988). San Diego Suicide Study III. Relationships between diagnoses and stressors. *Arch Gen Psychiatry, 45*: 589-592.

Rich, C.L., Young, D. & Fowler, R.C. (1986). San Diego Suicide Study: I. Young vs. Old Subjects. *Arch Gen Psychiatry, 43*:577-582.

Robbins, E., Murphy, G.E. Wilkinson, R.H., Gassner, S.Y. & Kayes, J. (1959). Some clinical considerations in the presentation of suicide based on a study of 134 successful suicides. *Am J Public Health, 49*:888-899.

Rutter, M., Grahm, P., Chadwick, O.F.D. & Yul, W. (1976). Adolescent turmoil: Fact or fiction? *J Child Psychol Psychiatry, 17*:35-57.

Sacco, W. & Graves, D. (1985). Correspondence between teacher ratings of childhood depression and self-ratings. *J Clin Child Psychol, 4*:353-355.

Schaffer, D. (1974). Suicide in childhood and early adolescence. *J Child Psychol Psychiatry, 15*:275-291.

Schaffer, D. & Fisher, P. (1981). The epidemiology of suicide in children and young adolescents. *The Journal, 20*:545-565.

Schaffer, D. (1985). *Suicide and depression in children and adolescents*. Presentation at the 7th Annual Adolescent Health Conference, Minneapolis, MN.

Schaffer, D. (1985). Completed Suicide Informant Interview. Unpublished manuscript, New York State Psychiatric Institute.

Schmidt, C.W., Perlin, S., Townes, W., Fisher, R.W. & Schaffer, J.W. (1972). Characteristics of drivers involved in single car accidents: A comparative study. *Arch Gen Psychiatry, 27*:800-803.

Schulsinger, F., Kety, S.S., Rosenthal, D. & Wender, P.H. (1979). A Family Study of Suicide. In: M. Schou, & E. Stromgren (Eds.) *Origin, Prevention, and Treatment of Affective Disorder*. New York: Academic Press, 278-287.

Shaffi, N., Carrigan, S., Whittinghill, J.R. & Derrick, A. (1985). Psychology autopsy of completed suicide in children and adolescents. *Am J Psychiatry, 142*:1061-1064.

Stack, S. (1986). Youth suicide rates. *American Association of Suicidology Newslink, 12*:6.

Thompson, T.R. (1987). Childhood and adolescent suicide in Manitoba: A demographic study. *Can J Psychiatry, 32*:264-269.

U.S. Department of Health, Education, and Welfare (1973): *Suicide, Homicide, and Alcoholism Among American Indians: Guidelines for Help*. Publication No. (ADM) 74-42. Rockville, MD.

Weisman, M., Orraschel, H. & Padian, N. (1980). Children's symptoms and social functioning self-report scales; comparison of mother's and children's report. *J Nerv Ment Dis, 168*:736-740.

Winn, M. (1983). *Children Without Childhood*. New York: Penguin.

BIOGRAPHICAL NOTE

Dr. Harry M. Hoberman graduated from Brown University in 1977 with an AB in Political Theory and Psychology. He received his MS and PhD in Clinical Psychology from the University of Oregon. He is currently an assistant professor of psychiatry and pediatrics at the University of Minnesota Medical School and serves as the Mental Health Specialist with the Adolescent Health Program. Dr. Hoberman directs clinical services for adolescents who are depressed or suicidal and those with eating disorders. His professional interests are studying the varied risk factors for adolescents who are depressed, suicidal or have eating disorders. In addition, he is interested in the application of time-limited treatments for adolescent psychopathology.

The Fairfax County
Suicide Prevention Program:
A Public School System Responds

Myra Herbert, MSW

Fairfax County, Virginia is a large suburb of Metropolitan Washington, D.C. It extends over an area of 400 square miles and encompasses numerous smaller self-contained communities that vary greatly in character. It is the heart of the Northern Virginia Region, a nine county coalition that for statistical and planning purposes is often viewed separately from the rest of the Commonwealth which is more rural with a lesser population density.

Families reside largely in single-family homes, although there are an increasing number of high-rise apartments and condominiums in the more urbanized areas. Low income and subsidized housing are rare, but there are a few small pockets of both. The county is culturally and economically mixed and the range extends from very poor to very wealthy. The largest percentage of the population is white middle-class and upper-middle-class. There has been a sizable influx of Southeast Asians who now make up 9.6% of the population, and more recently a growing number of Hispanic families who total 4.6% of the population. Blacks make up another 9%.

The county has experienced one of the most rapid growth rates in the United States in the past seven years and the boom continues, bringing with it the ensuing problems. In 1987 the county population was 704,757 and growing, with a median family income of $59,700. Studies of adolescent suicide across the North American continent indicate that just such affluent, middle-class communities

---

Myra Herbert is Coordinator, School Social Services, Fairfax County Public Schools, Fairfax, VA.

89

are apt to have a higher incidence of suicidal behavior in the adolescent population.

The school system is the tenth largest in the country with 182 schools and a student population of over 131,000 in the 1987-88 school year. There are more than 14,000 adults on the payroll, making it the largest employer in the county. The bus fleet is greater than that of most American cities. The total school budget exceeds $800,000,000. The community itself is educated, cosmopolitan, sophisticated and success-oriented.

In the 1980-81 school year there were eleven recorded adolescent deaths by suicide among students in Fairfax County schools. In addition to these eleven, there were a number of deaths recorded as accidental either because of the circumstances or because of the wishes of the families. There were also a number during the summer vacation or immediately after graduation. The actual total of deaths in the fifteen to nineteen-year old age group was at least twenty and perhaps higher.

In the 1982-83 school year, in response to the statistics of the previous year, the Fairfax County School Board elected to make suicide prevention program an annual operating plan priority and requested that the effort be organized to make it a cooperative school and community program. The Fairfax County Public Schools Department of Student Services and Special Education, an umbrella department that encompasses a wide range of related services, rapidly organized a school/community advisory committee with representation from the school system, the community mental health centers, the medical association, the mental health association and the police department. This committee served not only as an advisory committee, but took part in the implementation of the program, organizing speakers and contributing expertise.

The committee began its effort by searching for an existing model that had been used successfully in other school systems. At that time there were none to be found and the advisory group set about constructing one of their own. With the growth of national interest in the subject of adolescent suicide, several other excellent programs have been designed in other communities; the Fairfax County Program has, however, been accepted nationally as a model for many school systems, perhaps because it has been school initiated. Many of the other programs have been designed in the community, usually by mental health facilities, and have been brought into schools from outside agencies.

The cooperation of school and community agencies is not always easy to affect. School systems tend to be cautious and sometimes territorial and community agencies often do not recognize the demands and strictures placed on school personnel. Frequently there is a misunderstanding of the limits of a school system's power to put any kind of program in place without the support of the parent body of the school population. In a county as large as Fairfax, there are many different voices to be heard and political concerns cannot be overlooked.

The design agreed upon the first year was to deliver an awareness program to faculties, parents, and students of the high schools in the county. This was extended to the intermediate schools the second year of the program. In addition to an awareness effort each school would be asked to have a reliable system of referring children to counselling resources within and without the school. Practicality became the next problem. Sessions for teachers had to be held within contract hours but could not interfere with the proscribed school schedules or with daily responsibilities to students. The method decided upon was to hold informational sessions during designated faculty meetings and an open house in some comfortable area of the school during the following day. The awareness sessions were designed to describe the signs and symptoms of depressive and suicidal behavior in young people, particularly those that teachers would be most likely to recognize; to offer guidelines for talking with troubled children, and to offer methods for getting such children the necessary help they need. Staff was to be invited to drop in for discussions any free period during the school day when the open house sessions were held.

Meanwhile, members of the committee also screened appropriate audio-visual materials for use in the schools, researched bibliographies, and collected suitable literature to be distributed to all personnel. A speakers bureau was organized with voluntary contributors from school mental health personnel, community agencies and private practitioners. The representatives from the community mental health centers took the responsibility of creating a speakers bureau and connecting speakers to groups requesting them. The Northern Virginia Mental Health Association agreed to coordinate the organization of parent meetings that might take place during the school day and therefore require locations to meet outside the schools.

The entire program was launched with an address to senior administrators by the Chief of Psychiatry at Children's Hospital National Medical Center. Training sessions were then held for the social workers, psychologists, and guidance staff who would conduct or arrange faculty training sessions and who would be responsible for arranging referral channels in each school. The faculty training sessions varied greatly with each school. In some schools principals and vice principals were very invested in the program and took an active part in the planning. In others it was delegated to designated staff members. It proved to be true that the more involved the principal, the more involved the faculty and consequently, the more successful the program. The division superintendent sent out a memorandum to all schools requesting that such arrangements be made for awareness sessions and for constructing referral channels. At the same time letters were mailed to all Parent/Teacher organization chairpersons asking that their membership arrange a session on adolescent suicide prevention as near as possible to the one given at their school. They were also informed about speakers and supplementary material as well as other resources available to them. Schools were requested to conduct appropriate and useful information sessions for their students.

There is nothing more difficult to evaluate than a prevention program. The variables are endless and the findings may be completely coincidental. The incidence of student suicides dropped to five the first year of the program, fell to three the second year when the intermediate schools were included, and did not rise to above five until the 1987-88 school year. In that year there were nine recorded deaths and at least two more strongly believed to be suicides. The school system also experienced a cluster with three of these eleven deaths occurring in the same school and one in a private school in the same community. One death is too many, but the most stringent efforts are unlikely to eradicate completely suicide in our teenage population.

Plaudits go to school personnel and particularly to the teaching personnel. They have muttered and grumbled when given yet another task but they have performed well. They have taken seriously the issue of identifying troubled students and have seen to it that such students reach adults who can provide them with needed help. We have been unable to record accurate statistics, but the guidance counselors, social workers and psychologists in the system informally report that referrals from teachers have roughly **quadrupled** in the past several years. Community mental health centers report that the number of adolescents seeking help from them has doubled and private practitioners report an increase in referrals from the schools. Whatever the figures, more children are being reached before they resort to desperate measures.

When the program was assessed at the end of the first two-year period, it was discovered that all faculties had received awareness programs, that many of the PTA's had conducted sessions for their memberships but that very few schools had tackled any kind of activity for students. Only one, Madison High School, had created a program that reached the entire student body. It became necessary to examine why and what emerged were two main reasons. The first was that schools are very busy places and often need "packaged programs" if they will accommodate additional responsibilities into the already full roster. The second salient reason was that many adults were still uncomfortable talking about suicide with young people. There lingers the fear that talking about suicide will encourage it and perhaps instigate unhealthy behavior. Students themselves handle the subject matter easily and often bring it up spontaneously, but it became necessary to identify a method of circumventing what appeared to be an obstacle for many adults. The result was to create activities that focused on social and emotional issues of adolescents, rather than on crisis. The initial model used was the Student Stress Program. A guidance counselor and a mental health professional gathered a group of successfully functioning students known to be coping with a variety of stress factors common for adolescents. These varied somewhat from one school to another, but there are some that are predictable. Family issues and changing family structure, moving, changing schools, academic pressures, learning disabilities, losses of various kinds, social choices, and uncertainties about the future were matters that most students wanted to discuss. They were also encouraged to share the coping mechanisms they used for dealing with stress themselves. After approximately six meetings this group gives a panel session for the student body and then for parents. The results seem to be greater understanding and communication, and students have appreciated being heard. Since this program was initiated all of the high schools have reproduced it or some variation of it and all have found it worthwhile. Far from being reticent, adolescents are most honest with their feelings and enjoy sharing them.

As the program has progressed, a suicide prevention component has been incorporated into the peer counseling curriculum, and more recently into the mental health aspects of the health education curriculum. A county task force was formed of personnel who had faced crises in their schools and who have constructed a set of guidelines for coping with emergencies in schools, both for suicides and for related situations where the same precepts hold for communicating with the student body and with the community. In the 1987-88 school year it was required of all schools to have a written plan for crisis management.

Such plans include directions for personnel responsibility, announcements, space, group management and communication. When the suicide cluster occurred in the fall of 1987 the Department of Student Services and Special Education sought the advice of a child and adolescent psychiatrist, who studies adolescent suicide, and worked cooperatively with the school to develop emergency measures. The school system requested auxiliary assistance from the private practitioners in the entire Fairfax County mental health community. The response was generous and immediate. An interview protocol was designed and in-depth assessments were done on students felt to be at greatest risk because of their acquaintance to two or more of the deceased, and in some cases because of their own histories. A significant number of students were referred for professional help and several students were hospitalized. Follow-up, including individual attention and groups, continued with this population for the duration of the school year.

In addition, school personnel held discussions with the executive editor of the *Washington Post* and later with the *Post* reporters and editors about the manner in which the press reports on issues that affect children. As a result that newspaper has curtailed detailed and dramatic reporting of adolescent suicide and has taken a role in eliciting similar cooperation from other newspapers and also television and radio news bureaus. Sigma Delta Chi, the professional journalists society, also helped organize a public forum where a variety of views could be openly discussed. This, too, mitigated the sensationalizing of such news. Since many smaller newspapers and TV stations take material directly from those in major U.S. cities, and since it is now well-known that teens identify with and emulate what they read and view about their peers, this was regarded as a positive advance in prevention.

During the 1988-89 school year the school-team is emphasizing cooperation and the furthering of school and community agency integration. As the population of the county grows, Fairfax is experiencing an urbanization that seems to bring with it problems that are new in nature to what has been a relatively quiet suburban residential community. Social workers, psychologists and guidance counselors are pooling their skills and resources and using them optimally. Rather than concentrating on suicide and depression alone, school staff are constructing programs concerning students-at-risk. That is a blanket term meant to encompass the myriad issues we see with young people that often seem to drive some to the point of despair.

Although successful we are not complacent. As our children pass through our schools their problems change and the child who may have been coping well one year may have trouble the next. Each developmental stage brings new challenges. We are a transient society and must remain aware that our population is constantly moving and that uprooting brings losses and a barrage of other problems. It is awareness that helps us weave a safety net for our children and affords them support. Prevention begins with an understanding of the society in which we have placed our young, in its good and its harmful aspects and of its constantly changing forces. It is our responsibility to translate that understanding into working programs that help our young toward a healthy future.

REFERENCES

1. 1987 Fact Book (Fairfax, Va., Fairfax County Public Schools, 1987).
2. The 1987 Sourcebook of County Demographics (Arlington, VA, CACI, 1987).
3. Fairfax County Office of Research and Statistics.
4. Hodgkinson, Harold L., Fairfax County: Its Educational System in Context.

BIOGRAPHICAL NOTE

Myra Herbert has a Master's Degree in psychiatric social work and has been working with children and families, in teaching hospitals and schools for more than twenty years, both in the United States and England. She has held faculty positions in the medical schools at the University of Maryland, Johns Hopkins, University of London and George Washington University.

She became Chief of Social Work Services in Fairfax County Public Schools, the tenth largest system in the country with more than 131,000 children, in December 1980. The following year she was asked by the School Board to begin a school/community prevention program for adolescent suicide that has received national attention and is now viewed as a model for schools across the United States.

The Components of School-Based Suicide Prevention

Barry D. Garfinkel, MD, FRCP(C)

INTRODUCTION

As the statistics on high school student suicide rise dramatically, prevention of adolescent suicide has become a priority of professionals involved with our schools. Suicide prevention centers, crisis hotlines, family physicians, and teachers are just some of the different community resources available to help the suicidal individual. The efficacy of these various individuals and programs has, however, been subject to question. Controversy continues about whether or not suicide prevention centers and agencies, psychologists and psychotherapists can actually prevent suicide (Bagley, 1968; Sainsbury and Barraclough, 1968; Barraclough, Jennings and Moss, 1978; Innes, 1980). Overall however, suicide prevention centers may show some beneficial effects, especially by diminishing the rate of suicide in young white females (i.e., women and girls 24 years of age or younger).

Recently, suicide prevention programs and curricula have been developed for junior and senior high schools. These programs have assumed various tasks, but have as their overall goal the prevention of suicide of the students enrolled in school. All of the programs

Barry D. Garfinkel is Director of the Division of Child and Adolescent Psychiatry, Box 95, University of Minnesota Hospital and Clinic, Harvard Street at East River Road, Minneapolis, MN 55455.

This article is based on a presentation, "School-Based Prevention Programs," given at the National Conference on Prevention and Intervention in Youth Suicide, at Oakland, CA, June 1986, and was supported by NIMH Contract No. 278-85-0026(OD).

Report of Secretary's Task Force on Youth Suicide. Volume III, Prevention and Interventions in Youth Suicide (1989) Washington, D.C., U.S. Government Printing Office, *Alcohol, Drug Abuse* and *Mental Health Administration*.

currently utilize some of the functions of a comprehensive school-based prevention program. Unfortunately, there have been serious omissions in these programs. In reviewing this field, it is apparent that there are nine aspects of the prevention programs that must be developed to become part of the different school-based programs. They are:

1. early identification and screening;
2. comprehensive evaluation of the depressed, suicidal and psychiatrically disturbed young person;
3. crisis intervention and case management;
4. programs to be instituted immediately following a suicide;
5. education for students, teachers, community, and professionals on identification, diagnosis, and management of suicidal youth;
6. monitoring and follow-up;
7. community linkage and networking;
8. research of epidemiology, causation, and the longitudinal follow-up of attempters;
9. advocacy.

This paper will critically review the existing youth suicide prevention programs developed for schools and elaborate on some of the more critical aspects of the nine components of a systematic model that would provide an effective prevention program.

The general purpose of a successful school-based program should be to integrate an understanding of the risk factors for youth suicide, an appreciation of the behavioral characteristics and clinical symptomatology of the suicidal individual, and an awareness of the various psychosocial stressors with which the suicidal adolescent is attempting to cope. The synthesis of these various functions forms the basis of suicide curricula and programs conducted in schools currently.

EARLY IDENTIFICATION AND SCREENING

The question of "what is to be evaluated" arises in training educators and school administrative staff to screen for suicidal youth.

Does the screening include an examination for depression, antisocial behaviors and attitudes, impulsivity, suicidal intent, hopelessness, coping skills, family background and/or psychosocial stressors? Should it include all of these areas? Three general areas of early identification and screening must be examined:

1. depression in young people;
2. various psychosocial stressors affecting students;
3. their methods of responding to and handling difficult problems.

Early identification is dependent on the observance of the various risk factors that have been associated with suicide attempts and completed suicide in youth. Hawton (1982) has identified a number of risk factors as have Garfinkel, Froese, and Hood (1982). They are:

1. older adolescent
2. male
3. previous attempts
4. chemical dependency (alcoholism) in the family
5. family breakdown
6. deteriorating school performance
7. recent antisocial acts (characterized by rage, aggression, and impulsivity
8. living away from the family
9. prior history of depression

In a 1986 study of suicide attempts in high school students (Garfinkel et al., 1986) it was shown that attempters had more than twice the number of psychosocial stressors within a six month period prior to their attempts than non-depressed, non-suicidal adolescents. The various stressful events were not just more frequent but also were qualitatively distinct from the stressful events in non-attempters (Paykel, Prusoff and Myers, 1975). For example, family breakdown, divorce, and school-based difficulties were far more frequent in the attempters' group.

Common stressors experienced by the adolescent who attempted suicide include:

1. breakup with boyfriend or girlfriend;
2. trouble with brother or sister;
3. change in parents' financial status;
4. parental divorce;
5. losing a close friend;
6. trouble with teacher;
7. changing to a new school;
8. personal injury or other physical illness;
9. failing grades:
10. increased arguments with parents.

Although more than fifty events could be identified as upsetting to an adolescent, these ten were reported most often by the attempters. The stressful life events are listed in the order of frequency that adolescents attempting suicide identified as most to least stressful (Garfinkel et al., 1986).

The behavioral patterns and clinical features that characterize suicide attempters, in a high school setting, indicate behaviors not only associated with a particular *DSM-III-R* diagnosis or the criteria for depression, but they are also characterized by:

1. angry and explosive outbursts;
2. passive withdrawal into drinking, smoking, and drug usage;
3. avoidant types of behavior including hypersomnia, joyriding, and infrequent communication with adults;
4. recent antisocial behaviors such as fighting, violent outbursts, stealing, and vandalism;
5. visits to family doctors concerning physical symptoms;
6. deteriorating school work.

Recently, Garfinkel, Hoberman, Parsons, and Walker screened 4,267 junior and senior high school students in rural Minnesota. They examined five symptom and behavioral areas which include:

1. depression;
2. antisocial behavior;
3. life stressors;
4. familial and demographic factors;
5. coping and adaptive strategies.

Hopelessness and nihilism were not evaluated. Information concerning suicide attempts, ideation, and impact of role models were also assessed and shown to be of importance in determining suicide attempts. Instrumentation for this type of screening and early identification is relatively simple and brief. Self-report questionnaires and rating scales were used and were the most efficient way of obtaining this information. The Beck Depression Inventory, Birleson Rating Scale for Depression, A-COPE, Johnson and McCutchen Life Events Questionnaire were shown to have validity. By applying this information to specific students, an individual undergoing severe stress can be identified. A pattern emerges that often resembles that of a suicidal adolescent with a sufficient number of preexisting risk factors to warrant a further comprehensive evaluation.

COMPREHENSIVE EVALUATION

Following the application of screening measures, some students will be identified as in need of further evaluation. The comprehensive assessment and evaluation of a student attending a junior or senior high school must be based on a structured systematic psychiatric protocol. This should include a structured psychiatric diagnostic interview, self and clinician ratings, and psychometric testing. Parent and teacher ratings have also been found useful. The evaluation must utilize existing instruments that have a high degree of validity and reliability. Because the examination for depression reflects temporary and episodic states, most rating scales and instruments for evaluating depression do not have a high test-re-test reliability. There are, however, a number of structured psychiatric interviews that are effective in identifying depression and they include:

1. Kiddie-Schedule for Affective Disorders and Schizophrenia (K-SADS);
2. Diagnostic Interview for Children and Adolescents (DICA), (individual and parent);

3. Diagnostic Interview Schedule for Children (DISC), (individual and parent);
4. Children's Depression Rating Scale (CDRS)

Clinician ratings such as the Children's Depression Rating Scale demonstrate good psychometric properties. In addition, self-report rating such as the CDI (Children's Depression Inventory) Kovacs (1978), Birleson (1978) and Beck Depression Inventory, Beck (1979) are worthwhile for self rating of depression. Psychological tests such as the PIC (Personality Inventory for Children), the MMPI, and the Millon Personality Profile for Adolescents can be usefully applied to the evaluation of suicidal youth. Often in a school setting, the evaluation team must obtain both concurrent parental and teacher evaluations of the student and examine the difficulties being identified in as many settings as possible. Weinberg (1973) showed that between 40-60% of a group of learning disabled children were found to meet diagnostic criteria for depression. It is also useful to measure hopelessness and suicidal intent. Suicide intentions are measurable with instruments such as the Beck (Beck, Ward and Mendelsohn, 1961) or Pierce Scales (1981). The Beck Hopelessness Scale has been shown to be a very good predictor of completed suicide in individuals who have made a previous attempt (Beck et al., 1985).

CRISIS INTERVENTION – AN EIGHT STEP MODEL

Barteolucci and Drayer (1973) and Hawton and Catalan (1982) recommend a crisis intervention model based on brief, collaborative problem-solving therapy emphasizing the rapid resumption of control over one's environmental future. Various personnel inside and outside the school system may be effective in assuming a role in working with the crisis intervention team based within the school setting. The following individuals may provide help in conjunction with a consultation, liaison or a primary care model:

1. child and adolescent psychiatrist
2. school psychologist

3. nurse
4. social worker
5. teacher
6. principal
7. speech pathologist
8. occupational therapist
9. coach
10. audiologist
11. pediatric neurologist
12. clergy

Depending on the case, these diverse individuals may be asked to either consult or become a permanent member of the crisis intervention team. The role of psychotropic medication should be critically examined because it may be useful in being one part of treatment for the immediate crisis (Hawton and Catalan, 1982). In general, the purpose of the crisis team is to transform, for the depressed and suicidal adolescent, an environment that had precipitated the crisis. The team's goal is to provide a supportive, concerned, and empathic group of individuals and surroundings in school. The team must be prepared to work with the individual to alleviate psychological and social distress.

The school-based crisis team should have as one of its chief responsibilities the psychotherapeutic and social management of young people following a suicide attempt. It is important to establish immediately an integrated network of parents, community based professionals, school based educators, and counselors. Often the original crisis intervention work done with the school will determine how successful subsequent community-based counselling will be. If the rapport and therapeutic alliance established with the school-based personnel is effective, it is likely that community work will replicate that positive pattern. As outlined by Hawton (1982) and Beck, Schuyller, Herman (1974), there are a number of specific goals to accomplish during the crisis-intervention work with an adolescent who has attempted suicide. It has been demonstrated by Connell (1965), Catalan et al., (1980) Hawton, Gaths (1979), that all disciplines, including social workers, counselors, psychologists, nurses, and psychiatrists can evaluate the individual who has attempted suicide. They indicate that the diagnostic assessment of every adolescent need not involve only one discipline.

The goals of the assessment are as follows:

1. to establish a therapeutic alliance;
2. to determine the type of psychosocial stressors the individual had been experiencing;
3. to rule out the presence or absence of a psychiatric disorder;
4. to identify the adaptive and coping mechanisms that the individual uses to manage stress;
5. to determine all the external resources and support personnel within the individual's life that can be recruited to help;
6. to identify what further help the person is willing to accept, in order to stop the suicidal behavior.

The first step of this protocol is to determine all the events that immediately preceded the attempt. In general, a thorough history of the preceding 48 hours is essential. Events during the two days are reviewed with the individual to determine what was a precipitant or perceived by the individual as a reason for the self-destructive behavior. If no psychosocial stressors are identified and the suicide attempt has no obvious causation, it is very important that a psychiatric disorder be ruled out. Most often, when there are no apparent psychosocial stressors or obvious reasons for the self-destructive actions, the suicide attempt is directly an outgrowth of a serious psychiatric disorder, such as manic-depressive disorder or schizophrenia.

Next, an evaluation of the degree of hopelessness, suicidal risk, and dangerousness of the actions must occur. The circumstances of the attempt indicate how dangerous and serious the behavior was. Features that have been found by Garfinkel, Forese, and Hood (1982); Garfinkel and Golombek (1983); and Beck, Beck and Kovaks (1975) are important to identify in individuals:

1. whether others were near by;
2. the likelihood of being rescued;
3. the precautions taken to avoid discovery;
4. actions that indicate that death was likely (e.g., giving away one's most prized possessions;

5. intricate and extensive suicidal plans'
6. leaving a suicide note;
7. not telling others of the attempt following the self-destructive actions;
8. informing others of the attempt before it actually occurs;
9. family history of suicide.

Following an attempt it is useful to have the adolescent list and write down on paper, with the person doing the evaluation, all their current difficulties (Paykel, Prusoff and Myers, 1975). When listed in order of frequency, identifiable problems emerge and frequently they include the following:

1. problems with boyfriend or girlfriend
2. problems with parents
3. problems of non-specific nature within the family
4. problems that are school-based

Hawton, O'Grady et al. (1982), demonstrated a list of problem areas in 50 adolescents who had attempted suicide. Their problem areas were very similar, including: parental, school, peer, social, physical, sexual and alcohol based difficulties. It is important to note that such difficulties may in fact be a consequence of depression rather than a cause. They may also perpetuate a person's pessimistic view of himself and his future. Moreover, they may also have precipitated the crisis or the decision to end one's life.

Following the identification of existing problems and psychosocial stressors, the next step involves the identification of a psychiatric disorder. It is not only important to identify affective disorders but also cognitive problems as well. For children and adolescents it is known that individuals with learning disabilities and Attention-Deficit Hyperactivity Disorder have a high rate of depression. It is also known that individuals with depression have cognitive distortions and altered attributions that affect thought content. It is during this step that individuals completing the assessment have the ability to do a full mental status examination, emphasizing an evaluation of both mood and thought disorders.

The next component of the evaluation emphasizes the identification of family psychopathology, family dynamics, and external resources available to the individual. Research has indicated that significant psychopathology in family members, especially alcoholism and family breakdown are more frequently associated with adolescent suicide attempts. It is important to document general psychopathology in other family members and to note whether or not another family member has tried to commit suicide. Suicide attempts and completed suicide in other family members are associated with suicidal behavior in adolescents. Family dynamic issues are also important, especially in determining the help the young person will receive from individuals within the immediate environment. Because the family members coped with severe problems earlier, for a long period of time, they may not be helpful or empathic during the adolescent's present crisis; they may take a very rejecting, uncooperative attitude. They may also treat the child as if he/she were "expendable," i.e., the parents are so tired of the long-standing conflicts they have "given up" on the person's ever getting better. Without sufficient resources available to the attempter, closer types of intervention and observation such as day hospital and full hospitalization may be necessary.

The adaptive and coping mechanisms of the attempter should be explored. It is important to determine whether or not the attempter is showing the commonly observed behavior of individuals who may attempt suicide: passive withdrawal, avoidant behavior, irritable and angry responses, and impulsive/explosive antisocial actions. At this stage of evaluation, previous suicide attempts, ruminations, and plans should be identified. Finally, all supportive relationships must be identified which can include peers, family members, clergy, educators, and professionals. It is essential that the evaluator *not* establish strict confidentiality around the suicidal behavior. Promising to keep it secret and confidential, the clinician may exclude others observations of the youngster in all settings, which can ultimately lead to a fatality.

The last step is to establish a contract. The individual who has attempted suicide agrees for a specified period of time, usually three to four months, to work on specific problems with identified external resources without turning to suicide. Often, three to four months is necessary to allow for sufficient mood elevation, cognitive reorganization with new attributions, and the resolution of various psychosocial stressors to deter the individual from further suicidal behavior.

SURVIVING A CHILD AND ADOLESCENT SUICIDE

Following a suicide, educators and community workers have difficulty managing and counselling relatives, peers, and classmates of the individual who committed suicide. There are a number of principles that should be followed within the school setting that would deemphasize the role modeling that can occur following a suicide. All subsequent actions should be handled in a very sensitive manner deemphasizing but acknowledging the presence of guilt, responsibility, and anger. Two principles underlie this work: first, the need to prevent any social modeling from occurring, and second, to prevent negative feelings of guilt, responsibility, and anger to overwhelm the survivors.

A number of tasks must be undertaken in the school setting involving the school friends of the decedent and, in fact, the general student body. Following an attempt or completed suicide, usually at least one-third of the student body will hear about it. Educators must not assume that by discussing what has occurred, they are giving young people the idea of suicide as an option. The students can be encouraged to explore with adults the sense of loss and abandonment regarding the suicide of their classmate. Herzog and Resnik (1967) indicated that parents and peers may have difficulty in communicating openly about the individual who committed suicide and may need support, direct encouragement, and the opportunity and time set aside for discussing it.

Individuals working with peers of the decedent should attempt to stress the psychopathology that the individual was exhibiting. Other adolescents may have perceived the individual who committed suicide as not having had any problems whatsoever. Occasionally this is the case; however, more often the psychopathology was minimized or not readily apparent. Stressing the psychopathological elements in the individual's functioning demystifies the suicide, emphasizes the role of emotional and psychosocial disturbances, and makes it more difficult to identify with the dead individual. Work with the survivors should be directed toward breaking down and preventing identification with the individual who committed suicide. Stressing problems, emphasizing family situations unique to the individual, and deemphasizing the strengths the individual possessed are methods by which identifications can be diminished. Unique stressors affecting the individual should be identified and discussed with the other classmates. Emphasizing such psychosocial stressors as academic difficulties, breakup of peer relationships, physical illness, familial discord, gender identity problems, and emancipation issues that were stressful events in the individual's life places the suicide in the context of a set of circumstances unique to that particular individual. If the unique aspects are stressed, peers will have a more difficult time identifying with the decedent. Furthermore, professionals and educators working with the students should focus on depression and other stressors, rather than the death itself.

Peers, classmates, and family members should be encouraged to limit the extent of the memorialization being considered for the decedent. Although it has not been fully researched in a controlled fashion, there is some empirical evidence to suggest that individuals who memorialize a suicide do so much more elaborately than compared to a similarly aged person dying from other causes.

Finally, coming to terms with the loss and abandonment must be discussed. Survivors have great difficulty in comprehending this permanent and volitional action. These two particular (i.e., volitional and permanent) aspects of the decedent's actions should be discussed. In general non-specific communication models are not the most effective way of trying to limit the social modeling and the potential for clustering of suicides from occurring because broad and unfocused models require a great deal of ventilation of anger, over-identification with the decedent ("he was no different from the survivors"), responsibility and guilt.

EDUCATION

Many educational programs are available for students, teachers, and administrative school personnel to help develop sensitivity and awareness of the issues associated with youth suicide. Through the years, educational programs have varied in terms of their duration, content, and personnel. The major components of these various programs have included:

1. coping skills
2. prevention
3. intervention
4. postvention

Some programs have been as brief as one class period and others have grown to as many as three to six classes. No one has been able to demonstrate that these programs have had any direct benefit to students. Similarly, there is no evidence to suggest that programs for school personnel have been effective. It is possible, in fact, that general discussions of suicide may have a deleterious effect on students; the topic may inadvertently become idealized and appealing.

Garfinkel, Hoberman, Walker, and Parsons examined suicide educational programs in rural Minnesota high schools which were directed to either students or educational personnel to determine if these correlated with either the suicide attempt rate for a particular school or the occurrence of severe depression. Ten schools examined within six months had six suicide attempts. Beck Depression Inventories were completed on 200 students designated for this study. Students in grades 9, 10, 11, and 12 in a particular class were asked to fill out the Beck Depression Rating Scale, suicide information, demographic, coping, and life stress events schedules. Principals were then interviewed to determine the number of educational programs on suicide, depression, or stress that were provided in the school. They were also asked whether there were specific personnel within the school who were designated to give these educational programs and whether or not experts were brought in. The range of programs was rated on a scale from 0-4.

Whether or not educational programs were provided did not correlate with either the suicide attempt rate in a particular school or the occurrence or severity of depression recorded. The type of speaker by discipline, whether an outside expert or someone on faculty, did not influence the rate of suicide or the severity of depression. Similarly, the number of suicide education programs did not have a significant effect on these two variables. Neither the number of staff people nor the speaker's area of expertise had any effect.

This is a pilot study that will be replicated in a further forty schools. Criticism may be leveled at the fact that it was not known what philosophy or approach was being utilized in the programs. One can take heart in the fact these programs did not have an enhancing effect on the suicide and depression rate within the schools. Therefore, one can cautiously conclude from these preliminary findings that a non-standardized educational program within a school setting, directed to students and teachers, is not associated with an increase in suicide attempts or severe depression.

In addition, many of the educational models for students emphasize the need for more effective adaptation, coping skills, and communication among teenagers. Separate teacher instructions have been produced that deal with various aspects of depression and suicide. The most useful instruction emphasizes adaptation, i.e., coping skills, instead of focusing on the topic of suicide. Currently, it is not known whether it would be more helpful to discuss depression, coping mechanisms, or more effective communication and thereby avoid bringing the topic of suicide to the classroom and directly to the student's attention.

Most educational programs encourage the development of early self-recognition of depression. Techniques for detecting a tendency toward either depression or suicide in oneself and others would appear to be worthwhile skills to teach students. Examining ineffective coping styles, as well as the more effective coping mechanisms, is a very useful and practical educational program for students. Learning to deemphasize passive withdrawal, avoidant types of behaviors, alcohol and drug usage, angry and antisocial behaviors is also important. Emphasizing networking and the integration of adult guidance into the support system youth choose are worthwhile training skills for our high school students, as are reinforcing assertive and clear communication. Deemphasizing the rageful forms of communication and the indirect methods that are commonly seen in suicidal youth are also being brought to the attention of the students. At this time, it is not known whether educational programs emphasizing these issues will alter either coping or communication in depressed and suicidal individuals.

COMMUNITY LINKAGE AND NETWORKING

The school suicide prevention team can become a community link to other school districts, high schools, community mental health centers, hospitals, universities, churches, and private mental health practitioners; the legal system, including truant officers, probation officers, and community police officers frequently can be included; and community networking should include determining community wide educational programs. Networking will deal with the media and guide them to deemphasize the coverage of suicides and to establish follow-up, aftercare management, and treatment networks to serve young people after a crisis. Frequently the suicide prevention team within the school must interface with parents, siblings, children, and adolescents especially vulnerable to depression and suicide. The prevention team will work with youth in health, recreational, and social areas and in the exchange of expertise among all groups addressing this problem. The linkage serves as both a prevention, crisis intervention, and research base for the enhancement of the scientific and clinical knowledge about youth suicide.

RESEARCH

Applying the model outlined above, the University of Minnesota, Division of Child and Adolescent Psychiatry and the Agricultural Extension Program in the Department of Home Economics in association with the 4-H Clubs of Minnesota established a broad, community based study of youth suicide attempts in rural Minnesota. This study included 52 counties in three regions of rural Minnesota. It surveyed 82 schools and involved 65 agricultural extension agents. Over 4,267 students were surveyed and their information provided research on:

1. demographic characteristics of suicide attempters;
2. the prevalence of suicide attempts
3. stressful life events;
4. coping and adaptive skills;
5. a self-rating scale for depression;
6. a self-rating scale for hopelessness
7. an inventory of antisocial behaviors;

This type of research was only possible with the help of an extensive network of professionals working within the schools in collaboration with community resources. Extensive research of this type is possible by utilizing existing networks and teams in and outside of our junior and senior high schools.

MONITORING AND FOLLOW-UP

Because of the unique function of schools, which keep all children below the age of 16 in school full-time, eight hours a day, five days a week, students in junior high school and the early grades of senior high school are much more readily available for monitoring and follow-up purposes. Unlike children who have made a serious suicide attempt or gesture, the diversity of adults' vocational and social functioning makes it difficult to determine whether or not they are compliant with recommended management programs. Children and adolescents on the other hand can be followed within the schools by a suicide prevention team, as well as having the school team monitor community based treatment programs. Because the individual who attempts suicide is most at risk for ultimately completing suicide, it is imperative to monitor these individuals closely (Guze and Robins, 1970). Monitoring and supervising the progress, in the individual who has been identified either as at risk or following self-destructive behavior, can be a major function of the school based team. Similarly, this team is in a unique position to monitor community wide trends regarding suicide, community education efforts, media exploitation of youth suicide (Barraclough, Shephard and Jennings, 1977), recent advances in suicide research, and specific school trends over a number of years. Suicide in a particular school can be examined as a function of unique local situations and events.

CONCLUSIONS:
THE YOUNG PERSON'S ADVOCATE

The development of suicide prevention programs and teams within our junior and senior high schools has resulted in a number of programs being developed. These include:

1. early identification
2. comprehensive evaluation
3. crisis intervention
4. postvention
5. education
6. monitoring
7. community linkage
8. research

The provision of these different functions can be accomplished when the students are maintained within their routine and regular activities. The school program becomes a resource not only for the school and district, but for the entire community. It becomes a clearing house for new research, comprehensive management techniques, and the coordination of community education efforts in the area of suicide. Moreover, as this team monitors, follows up, and establishes a registry of individuals at highest risk for suicide, it can become the children's most effective advocates. School, peer, and parental attitudes may be insensitive and unaware of the depressed and suicidal individual who lacks the energy, social skills, and abilities to effectively deal with the usual adolescent developmental demands. Having advocates within the school setting can provide an explanatory immediate response to difficulties with teachers, peers, classmates, and parents. Clarifying to both teachers and parents that a suicidal and depressed individual may not be able to concentrate and complete homework and therefore, punitive actions about incomplete assignments, lack of energy, and excessive daydreaming may be harmful to an already depressed individual. Explaining physical ailments and somatic symptoms may also be very helpful. As the young person's advocate, the prevention team ultimately can recognize behavioral, physical, and social problems as occurring in more than one perspective. Rather than observing antisocial behaviors entirely within a conduct disorder framework, one can also present them as adaptive behaviors commonly seen in depressed and suicidal individuals.

The most important function of all is for the suicidal student to have an advocate readily available eight hours, five days per week to be knowledgeable about the thoughts and feelings the student is experiencing, to interpret more effectively the individual's behavior towards others, and to accomplish these tasks in an empathic fashion to the student. It is estimated between 3-6% of all high school students will require the direct services of a suicide prevention team (Shaffer and Fisher, 1981). Not only for students at risk, but all students, teachers, and members of the community will benefit from the diverse activities that have been outlined in this chapter.

REFERENCES

Bagley, C.R. (1968). The evaluation of a suicide prevention scheme by an ecological method. *Social Sciences and Medicine*, 2:1-14.

Barraclough, B.M., Jennings, C., & Moss, J.R. (1978). Suicide prevention by the Samaritans: a controlled study of effectiveness. *Lancet*, 2:868-870.

Barraclough, B., Shepherd, D., & Jennings, C. (1977). Do newspaper reports of coroners' inquests incite people to commit suicide? *British Journal of Psychiatry*, 19:523-527.

Bartolucci, G, & Drayer, C.S. (1973). An overview of crisis intervention in the emergency room of general hospitals. *Am J Psychiatry*, 130:953-960.

Beck, A.T., Steer, R.A., Kovacs, M., & Garrison, B. (1985). Hopelessness and eventual suicide: a ten-year prospective study of patients hospitalized with suicidal ideation. *Am J Psychiatry*, 142:559-563.

Beck, A.T., Beck, R., & Kovacs, M. (1975). Classification of suicidal behavior: I. Quantifying intent and medical lethality. *American Journal of Psychiatry*, 132:285-287.

Beck, A.T., Schuyler, R.D., & Herman, J. (1974). Development of suicidal intent scales. In: A. T. Beck, H.L.P. Resnick, & D.J. Lettieri (Eds.), *The Prediction of Suicide*. Illinois: Charles Press.

Beck, A.T., Ward, C.H., & Mendelson, M. (1961). An inventory for measuring depression. *Archives of General Psychiatry*, 4:561-571.

Catalan, J., Marsack, P., Hawton, K.E., Whitwell, D., Fagg, J., & Bancroft,

J.H.J. (1980). Comparison of doctors and nurses in the assessment of deliberate self-poisoning patients. *Psychological Medicine*, 10:483-491.

Connell, P.H. (1965). Suicidal attempts in childhood and adolescence. In: J.G. Howell (Ed.), *Modern Perspectives in Child Psychiatry*. Edinburgh: Oliver and Boyd.

Garfinkel, B.D. (1986). School-based prevention program. Unpublished paper presented at the National Conference on Prevention and Interventions in Youth Suicide. Oakland, CA.

Garfinkel, B.D., & Golombek, H. (1983). Suicidal behavior in adolescence. In: H. Golombek & B.D. Garfinkel (Eds.), *The Adolescent and Mood Disturbance*. New York: International University Press.

Garfinkel, B.D., Hoberman, H., Parsons, J, & Walker, J. (1986). Stress, depression and suicide: a study of adolescents in Minnesota. Proceedings from: Responding to High Risk Youth: A statewide interactive satellite video teleconference for adults who work with adolescents, unpublished data.

Guze, S., & Robins, E. (1970). Suicide and primary affective disorders. *British Journal of Psychiatry*, 117:437-438.

Hawton, K., & Catalan, J. (1982). *Attempted Suicide: A Practical Guide to its Nature and Management*. Oxford: Oxford University Press.

Hawton, K., Cole, D., O'Grady, J., & Osborn, M. (1982). Motivational aspects of deliberate self-poisoning in adolescents. *British Journal of Psychiatry*, 141:286-291.

Hawton, K., O'Grady, J., Osborn, M., & Cole, D. (1982). Classification of adolescents who take overdoses. *British Journal of Psychiatry*, 140:124-131.

Hawton, K., Gath, D., & Smith, E. (1979). Management of attempted suicide in Oxford. *Brit Med J*, 27:1040-1042.

Herzog & Resnick

Innes, J.M. (1980). Suicide and the Samaritans. *Lancet*, i:1138-1139.

Paykel, E.S., Prusoff, B.A., & Myers, J.K. (1975). Suicide attempts and recent life events: A controlled comparison. *Archives of General Psychiatry*, 32:327-333.

Sainsbury, P., & Barraclough, B. (1968). Differences between suicide rates. *Nature*, 220:1252.

Shaffer, D., & Fisher, P. (1981). The epidemiology of suicide in children and young adolescents. *Journal of the American Academy of Child Psychiatry*, 20:545-565.

Weinberg, W.A., Rutman, J., Sullivan, L. et al. (1973). Depression in children referred to an educational diagnostic center: Diagnosis and treatment. *J Pediatr*, 83:1065-1072.

BIOGRAPHICAL NOTE

Dr. Barry D. Garfinkel is Director of the Division of Child and Adolescent Psychiatry. Dr. Garfinkel has been with the University of Minnesota for six years. Previously, he was with the Department of Psychiatry at Brown University where he was Director of Graduate and Undergraduate Medical Education in child psychiatry. He received his medical degree at the University of Manitoba and training in adult and child and adolescent psychiatry at the University of Toronto. He completed his child and adolescent psychiatry training in 1974 at the Hospital for Sick Children, Toronto.

Dr. Garfinkel's clinical and research interests are in the areas of depression and suicide in children and adolescents, anxiety and obsessive-compulsive disorders, pharmacological research in children and adolescents with Attention Deficit Disorder. He is currently studying suicide risk factors in youth, the prevalence of suicide, and suicidal communication. Other research includes the metabolism of Ritalin, the Epidemiology of Attention Deficit Disorder (ADD) and the computer assisted assessment of children and adolescents.